Managing to Care:
Public Service and the Market

Consultant Editor: Jo Campling

Managing to Care: Public Service and the Market

Ann James

Longman
London and New York

Longman Group Limited
Longman House, Burnt Mill,
Harlow, Essex CM20 2JE, England
and Associated Companies throughout the world.

Published in the United States of America
by Longman Publishing, New York

© Longman Group Limited 1994

First published 1994

ISBN 0 582 23965 6 PPR

British Library Cataloguing-in-Publication Data

A catalogue record for this book is
available from the British Library

Library of Congress Cataloging-in-Publication Data
James, Ann, Ph. D.
   Managing to care : public service and the market / Ann James.
      p.   cm.
   Includes bibliographical references (p.   ) and index.
   ISBN 0-582-23965-6
   1. Great Britain--Social policy--1979– 2. Human services--Great
Britain--Management. I. Title.
HN385.5.J36   1994
361.941--dc20   94-15824
                                                                 CIP

Set by 7 in 10/12 Bembo
Printed in Malaysia

Contents

Acknowledgements

This book is for Brian Caul, my first line manager, and Neil Leighton, who first taught me the difference between management and professional practice.

Thanks go to Jo Campling and Paul Snell, who consistently persuaded me I had something worth saying on the subject, and to my friends at the University of Birmingham, especially Nicholas Deakin and Neil Thomas, who gave me a platform from which to say it.

Much appreciated for their imaginative and thoughtful comments on my first draft are Martin Fischer, Mike Lauerman, Tim Dartington, David Towell and my brother, Clarence Schofield, for his encouragement. Thank you to Saroj Purba for translating my scribbles into text without fuss, and most of all thank you Rebecca, Eliza and Ben who put up with the moans, groans and self-doubt and jubilation that is every writer's lot.

Ann James

The publishers are indebted to the Institute of Management for permission to reproduce the BIM strategy statement, September 1987.

CHAPTER ONE

Managing to care

Margaret Thatcher did Britain two favours. First, the scale, speed and consistency with which she applied her policies in the public sector created the potential for nothing less than a paradigm shift in thinking about delivery of human services. Second, she ceased to be prime minister at a point at which the process of implementing that paradigm shift was incomplete and therefore both process and outcomes were still malleable. The challenge of the 1990s is one of using the space created by Thatcher's paradigm shift, at least to improve service and service delivery, at most to help build healthy communities.

Starting first with the notion of building healthy communities is in itself something of a *volte-face*. It assumes that managing welfare is no longer managing something that is state-provided and user-received. Rather that it is about managing the empowerment process at the national and local levels such that communities can themselves begin to respond to what they see as identified need, whether or not that response is in the form of service provision.

Empowerment in this sense, which literally means 'investing with power', needs to be distinguished from other meanings which the term has taken on as a result of certain political and social constructions. These include using empowerment as a moral imperative (a 'good thing'); using it as a survival strategy for obsolete organisations; or using it, as professionals and managers occasionally do, when what they really mean is paternalism.

People who are ill or who have disabilities, people who are very old or very young, people who are unemployed or who live in poverty, people who are uneducated, or homeless, and people who care for them, people who have offended against the law: these are the people who make up the majority users of our care services.

Managing service provision and procurement for these people may be similar to managing other sorts of services, but it is not the same. It is not the same because managing public service in general and welfare services in particular is about serving a particular clientele or a particular market segment. Some of that clientele, that market segment, has been chronically deprived of basic human rights over generations. For others, the act of presenting themselves for service is a single but nonetheless dependent act. For others again, it is a reluctant and chronic situation; a function of age, disability or circumstance.

Managing this clientele is therefore not about how to control but how to enable, not how to maximise profit but how to enfranchise. Empowerment of users is not a bolted on extra to managing welfare, but central to it.

Politics (that is, the use and abuse of power) is also central to the management process. The essence of managing in a political arena is not one of managers managing politicians or politicians managing managers and of both managing professionals but of continually improving representation from users, non-users and potential users in the community such that decisions can be made and acted upon with legitimacy. This is a political process. It has traditionally been associated with the role of elected members of the community and indeed this has proved relatively successful. (The variation between budget allocation and utilisation among relative services across local authorities indicates not, as popularly conceived, poor management and resource abuse, but rather, local variety and with it, local images of justice.)

What Thatcher tried to do was that required by the market economy, namely force the pace in separating the function of representation from the process of local election. This separation was already emerging. Communities were already finding representation through other means, a situation to which declining attendance at the ballot box testified. These means included pressure groups, advocacy groups, large public meetings, the media, complaint, and ultimately, riot. The problem with these means was that they confused voice with representation and representation with equity. Meanwhile, for Thatcher, alliances with users or with their direct representatives was at one and the same time a way of vote-catching while disempowering troublesome elected members at the local level. The creation of boards in public services in imitation of boards of shareholders was, simultaneously, a way of managing public voice safely and a way of removing the stranglehold of the elected official. So, for example, parents were given governor status in schools, and non-executive directors were appointed to health boards.

The separation of the function of representation from the process of local election is helpful in that it separates means from ends. However, the notion of shareholding as an alternative mechanism to elected representation is itself flawed since as yet the status of shareholder is one that continues to elude most of the users of our public services. This will continue to be the case as long as fundamental inequalities exist in the areas of race, gender and disability. For these inequalities continue to legitimate inequality, and as such promote it in other parts of the United Kingdom social system. It is for this reason that equal opportunities, like politics, is intrinsic to the management process of welfare services.

Building appropriate welfare services must involve building those appropriate to the communities they represent. Chapter 2 of this volume outlines some of the changing features of those communities. These included changes to the social structure (to the family, to gender patterns, to employment patterns and to multiracial living); to economic behaviour (including an acceptance of resource constraint); technological advancement (including the management of information and access to it), and above all, a revised set of values. The removal from power of Thatcher was due in some part to her failure to appreciate the level of public support for collective action in the field of health and welfare. This was not collective action on the scale of Beveridge, or even Titmuss, but simply commitment to a certain level of equality in a world that was fundamentally unequal. She confused this justice-oriented set of ends with what she perceived as resistance to the means of implementation, namely the mixed economy. In fact communities were increasingly supportive of the mixed economy, as the Labour Party conceded in the early 1990s, when it too learned to separate ends from means and conceded the social market. But Thatcher's simplistic free market model had reduced every transaction to that of the grocer's shop, between an individual purchaser and provider, and falsely separated economic from political intent (Leadbeater 1991). This was seen in its most naked form in the Health Service reforms.

The market simply followed money. What Thatcher failed to acknowledge was the political responsibility, based on public consent, to place money such that the market was managed to achieve ends which together were more than the sum of a series of individual transactions. This was a lesson rapidly learned by the early Trust hospitals, opted-out schools and fundholding GP practices.

The emergence of the European Community as a force for social justice and social responsibility was rightly seen by Thatcher as a major threat to her views. The economic success of the social democratic-style state (notably Germany, Japan and Canada) was in contrast to the overt failure of both the free market (as in the United States) and the planned

3

economy (the Eastern bloc). The answer lay in some combination. The early 1990s saw the repeated emergence of more right-wing governments in Western Europe within a limited band of political expression. The UK was no different in this respect with the 1992 Conservative election victory.

The concepts of the social market and later, under Major's premiership, the Citizens' Charters, emerged in the early 1990s not as political theory or sets of practices, but initially as political slogans designed to pick up on the flip side to Thatcherism. They were reinforced by world recession in free market and planned economies alike. The ideas were ripe for their time. Leadbeater argued for a social market which would utilise a contract economy, but within the whole network of responsibilities and obligations that has traditionally made up the fabric of community life. These responsibilities and obligations have traditionally been associated either with families or with an interventionist state at local or national level. In a post-Fordist era, (chapter 4), public and private are woven together so that the source of service delivery becomes much less important than its quality and its outcome. Companies and schools can contribute alongside town halls. Consumers can contribute alongside professionals.

Thatcher's premiership and her subsequent removal from office, gave Britain the opportunity to operate in a world made up of neither hierarchical, professional nor market organisations. Public service no longer needs to correlate with hierarchy. Private no longer needs to be the opposite of public, nor professional that of management. Pluralism does not have to exclude individual initiative, nor democracy professional discretion. Information about the needs of communities no longer has to be organisationally specific. Indeed, organisations can themselves be simply nodules on a network that is itself the community. The paradigm shift is in the mind of the perceiver.

So what kind of managers are required to manage the kind of organisations that will promote empowerment of communities? First of all, they practise principled management.

There was much talk in the 1980s about value-driven management. For a while value-driven management was presented as if it were an alternative to private sector management and the key characteristic of public sector management (Stewart 1986). Later it became an excuse for not going along with environmental change in the form of a managed market economy. Still later it became a retreat: as long as we talked about values we could assume that different agencies, different professions, different levels of staff, agreed with each other at some fundamental level. Words like 'empowerment', 'user', normalisation', 'community', took on new social constructions such that consensus could be seen to be achieved

4

without any really serious challenge either to ways of working or of perceiving the world.

The best example of this is the term 'community care', which for the Health Service meant deinstitutionalisation of the chronic sick, a specific term to distinguish it within the Health Service from primary care and social care. But for Social Services, community care meant all those things and much more besides. Taking its origin from the community development movement in social work of the late 1960s, it was a discipline, a way of working with its own values and methods. Health and Social Services were using the same language, but with different meanings.

So the exercises undertaken by organisations, clusters of organisations and parts of organisations to identify core values were less to do with values than with assuming consensus, for indeed real conflict of values can never be resolved. What the exercises did do however, and why they were so successful in process terms, is that they brought people together to listen to each other, and that is very important to organisations in change. The platitudinous nature of the core values, once translated onto paper, confirmed that it was the process rather than the outcome that was valued. Indeed core values constructed in this way were in practice very little used by staff or managers other than for flag-waving or inspection purposes.

It is important to separate these exercises in value-setting from principled management, which takes values as a given and uses the process of management to implement them. This goes back to a point made earlier in the chapter, that if you take values such as commitment to users, equal opportunity and political representation seriously, you end up with a different kind of management than if you don't. What that means is that the way you do business is as important as the business that you do. That may not mean that all decisions are the most efficient in short-term economic terms, but that they are efficient in representation terms, and being so, will stick in the longer term.

Equal opportunities, for example, is not an extra, but intrinsic to the value set and therefore expressed, not just in policies for users but in everyday behaviour of staff to each other. For welfare has a different function to capitalism. Welfare comes in where capitalism fails. There is no sense therefore in welfare competing with the same mind set as capitalism. The aim of welfare is not economy, though the means is quite appropriately curtailed by economics and there may be outcomes to the welfare process which are economic, such as a fit and educated workforce. The aim of welfare, in the UK at least, is to ameliorate the effects of capitalism.

It follows therefore that management in this model is not a top-down control process, but management by empowerment of staff and users. Again that is not to be confused with decentralisation, which may or may not be empowering depending on whether the resources which are decentralised are real or imagined and whether accountability and responsibility are revised in line with resource delegation. For there is no empowerment in giving away a spent budget or one dominated by a fixed staff establishment. Indeed while structural reorganisation can create the illusion of empowerment, the destabilisation it causes can in turn lead to contrary outcomes. Delegating power that is unreal or not understood feels like dumping to the delegated.

Management by empowerment has rather different characteristics. First of all it questions the traditional distinctions between first-line, middle and senior managers. These distinctions are a leftover of old-style hierarchical institutions combined with traditional images of status and privilege. The hierarchical model sees first-line managers as 'foremen' (in the old gender typology), that is, senior practitioners whose function it is to be able to advise and supervise more junior practitioner staff. They are the 'player-managers'. It sees the senior managers as strategic thinkers, whose business it is to care for the organisation's purpose and values and outcomes as a whole. And it sees the middle managers as managing operations.

In fact this no longer represents what happens in practice. The evidence is that senior managers, often ex-professionals, find it difficult to keep out of operations. And as far back as 1988 first-line managers in Social Services were found to undertake a very extensive and varied range of activities which appeared to be appropriate more to professionals or senior managers than to supervisors (James 1988). As for middle managers, their experience is less one of managing operations than of bridging the gap between first line and senior managers. They do everything that senior managers and first-line managers don't do. They are the jam in the sandwich; the movers and fixers in the organisation, who are forced to innovate or burn out. For their position makes it impossible for them to manage the degrees of change being passed down from senior managers and passed up from first liners. The assistant chief probation officers and mature senior probation officers are a case in point. Without a clear role themselves, they are forced to identify with either the chief probation officer or the senior professional probation officer.

The problem could be construed as one of role confusion, and indeed has been on many occasions within individual organisations. However, the very scale of the disjunction between the theory and praxis indicates a much simpler explanation. It may be that the hierarchical divisions of management have more to do with a professional and bureaucratic heritage than with management processes. It may be that they owe more to ways of carving up staffing according to the division of labour, and with them, appropriate conditions to service and pay, than to management practice (chapter 4).

In practice, strategic management seems to happen at all levels, though it is certainly logged, catalogued and is influential at senior level. To understand this means thinking again about the notion of strategic management as something which may involve strategic thinking, may involve strategic planning, but above all involves strategic action (chapter 5). Separating operations, or actions, from strategy is a product of Taylor's (1911) separation of process from monitoring and control (chapter 4). This is not necessarily an accurate representation of management in practice in which most actions emerge as strategic only with hindsight. We look back and can trace the actions and decisions which took us down one path rather than another, though those actions and those decisions may or may not have appeared significant at the time. So strategy is something emergent rather than given (Mintzberg 1983), incremental rather than a ground plan (Quinn 1980).

Similarly operational management is not a task confined to middle management and therefore of lower status. Maybe senior managers get involved in operations because that is what management is. It is not just a planning exercise, it is not just a thinking exercise, it is above all an activity. The only good managers are those who ultimately get things done, not those who sit in offices and think about them.

Neither is staff supervision a task confined to first-line managers. Maybe again, the reason that first-line managers act as Jack/ Jill-of-all-trades is that that is exactly what they are.

What we are talking about is management not by horizontal division or status, but about vertical strategic management, about vertical operations management and about vertical staff management. Management by empowerment now starts to take on a whole new meaning. We no longer talk of delegation, of giving power away. Management becomes the process by which ideas, activities, intentions are brought together to produce agreed and principled outcomes. Those ideas, those activities, those intentions may occur at any level. The task of the empowering manager is to enable ideas to happen or to recognise them when they occur, ensure ownership of them is retained, select from them, and help convert them into practice.

Talk of innovatory practice, talk of product champions, talk of managing up and across as well as down now begins to make sense. The empowering manager is the one who creates the conditions under which innovation can happen. That means setting up mechanisms to listen to staff, and learning from failure as well as success. It means enabling others to pursue the limelight with an idea or a process or an activity to which they are passionately committed, provided of course that it fits with organisational intentions. It means managing staff second-hand, that is, across line management or organisational boundaries but not second-rate. It means a capacity for managers to move in and out of hierarchies and in and out of markets; indeed to manage their constant entry and exit into a whole range of organisational situations in order to facilitate required outcomes.

This is not a model of leadership as popularly conceived. The 'new public manager' (Hood 1991) is something like a pop star manager. Very much like the mythical 'total women' of the 1970s, this manager is supposed to combine the capacity to work at peak for long hours for long periods, with personal accessibility, acute financial acumen, a certain degree of ruthless careerism, and above all personal charm and charisma.

Everybody needs stars. Large organisations need them badly, especially when times are hard. Hollywood flourished, after all, in response to a wartime experience. Stars are a good idea, but only if they can manage as well as star. The issue for the new managers is not how to be driven by the market rather than driven by the bureaucracy. The issue is rather how to be driven by the user. What that requires are organisations and managers which are flexible, responsive and who listen and are accountable to what they hear.

So, how do we move from one way of managing human services to another? First, certain structural prerequisites need to be in place. Community empowerment is not an alternative to state commitment. It only works if the environment is conducive. Those structural prerequisites are predictable and have and are being worked on at government level. They include mechanisms for funding and for political consent and representation, which take account of changes in demography, social structure, technology and the economy.

Second, a major attitude shift has to take place among users, the general public, politicians, and most of all, among staff of human service organisations. The shift is into believing that community empowerment is worth doing, and that it can be done. What that requires of staff is letting go of attachment to hierarchy and bureaucracy and professional paternalism. That in itself involves a grieving process which many have not yet acknowledged. It requires developing assertion and advocacy skill in users and educating them. It requires also generation of and adherence to an alternative vision of success, which is located not in the world of professionalism or of management or of politics, but in the real world of the user. Pressures from the environment will help that attitude shift come about, but only in part. Pressure from inside those human service organisations is equally important.

This is a chapter that looks back to the future. It asks what we have learned from our activities in health and social welfare and challenges us to take that learning with us. It asks awkward questions about the social meaning ascribed to some of the changes. And above all it seeks to map out, albeit haltingly and with reservations, some of the characteristics of the new management designed to empower communities. It does so with enthusiasm, with vision, but remember, without hindsight.

REFERENCES

Hood, C. (1991), 'A public management for all seasons', *Public Administration,* vol. 69, Spring 1991, pp. 3–19

James, A. (1988), *Managing to Care: A Study of First Line Managers in Day and Domiciliary Care,* London: HMSO

Leadbeater, C. (1991), 'Whose line is it anyway?', *Marxism Today,* July, pp. 20–22

Mintzberg, H. (1983), *Power in and Around Organisations,* Englewood Cliffs, NJ: Prentice-Hall

Quinn, J.B. (1980), *Strategies for Change: Logical Incrementalism,* Illinois: Irwin

Stewart, J. (1986), *The New Management of Locan Government,* London: Allen and Unwin

Taylor, F.W. (1911), *The Principles of Scientific Management,* New York: Harper

CHAPTER TWO

A changing environment

SUMMARY AND INTRODUCTION

Using a PEST analysis (i.e. analysing changes in Political, Economic, Social and Technological structures), chapter 2 charts the major changes taking place in the UK in the 1980s and early 1990s and offers a range of explanations for these based upon authoritative sources. It points out where these changes inform, or indeed contradict social policies as pursued by the government of the day. At the end of each section, key areas of potential concern to managers of public services are identified and discussed.

Broadly speaking, we get the kind of public services we deserve. For services, though they may seek to lead opinion, are a product of the people, the institution, the society, of their history and their times.

Whether we regard the events of the 1980s as evolution in the life of the welfare state, as a crisis, or indeed as its cessation (Mishra 1984), certainly by the end of the decade there was broad consensus among politicians, practitioners, managers and academics that services were, or were about to become, irrevocably different. The mixed economy of health and welfare was here to stay even if reluctantly in some quarters. Including within it a rich variety of views across the political spectrum about the position of the user, the accountability of officers and politicians and the relative value of induced market forces, it was broadly agreed that the mixed economy model would replace the centralist, statist provision of the post-war welfare state in health, welfare, education and other public services.

So what kind of people, what kind of institutions, what kind of society were to produce this major shift in welfare policy? An outline and analysis of the broad political, economic, social and technological trends of that decade are a prerequisite to any reply.

That is not of course to devalue in any way the heritage of care services management prior to the 1980s in the broader framework of shifting relations between personal social services and the state in the second half of the twentieth century (chapter 3). Rather it is to recognise that the job of the social policy-maker is to make policy, and that of the manager to manage. So whereas the social policy-maker needs a broad conceptual grasp of history and of chronology, the manager needs rather sufficient understanding of the relationship between the organisation and the environment to make appropriate decisions (i.e. information rather than data). Chronology is one way of representing those shifting relationships. Another is to examine them within a fixed time frame (here the 1980s) using a conceptual model. A PEST analysis is just such a model, designed to give the manager a broad grasp of the issues in a way that might promote both identification of those which are significant for the purposes of explanation, prediction or decision-making, and those which require further investigation. To use the colloquial, it is quick, but not necessarily dirty.

POLITICAL TRENDS

The 1980s and early 1990s saw attempts to apply free market principles to public service in the fields of housing, education, health, social services and the criminal justice system. It was, however, a solution not confined to the personal social services, finding expression concurrently in the BBC, the Post Office, British Rail, the CEGB and the vast majority of other publicly owned enterprises.

Comprising a set of fairly standard activities, though with an inconsistency of nomenclature, the market solution nonetheless depended upon the successful creation of a particular way of defining the nature of the problems besetting those organizations. Not that there were not very real problems in delivering service from an institutional base more appropriate to a post-war society than to Britain in the late twentieth century. Indeed those problems had themselves been catalogued in a number of ways by leading academics in social policy over the 1970s and were themselves being experienced by managers. But this broad analysis was now suddenly converted to legislative action which promoted the free market over collective solutions.

Why and how did this happen? Because the welfare state, it seems, was guilty on at least three counts. First welfarism itself, that particular ideology based on collective responsibility that emerged after the Second World War across the political spectrum, was apparently out of date. More than that, it was undesirable: for Thatcher reached back into an old liberalist tradition, of self-help and individual responsibility. For the Tories before Thatcher welfare statism had represented paternalistic care; a mechanism by which the haves looked after the have-nots and, in some cases, even justified that relationship. For the Labour party it was the natural outcome of socialist collective responsibility. But for Margaret Thatcher and the New Right, rolling back the role of state in welfare meant rolling back welfare as well as the state. In other words, it was not just statism that was rejected, but notions of welfarism itself. And so, during the 1970s and early 1980s welfare itself began to be attached to pejorative labels, beginning with the social construction of scroungers and ending with the attempt to dub community charge objectors as political extremists and militants. (In the end both labels failed to stick.) In this construction, social workers, to take an example, like teachers before them and probation officers after them, were often identified as namby-pamby do-gooders, who lacked either managerial competence or public credibility (a view all too often confirmed in practice it seemed according to the media). And so potential solutions, such as improved social work training and good public relations, became not solutions but themselves part of the problem and contributed to its complexity. Welfare it seemed, was a soft option.

Second, welfare, like education, the Health Service and indeed most if not all human service organisations, depended heavily on professionals. The effectiveness of applying market principles to personal social services depended crucially on either co-opting or crushing the power of professionals in order to facilitate managerial control. Professional clinicians in the Health Service had already demonstrated their power to frustrate general management principles. Thatcher's battle against the power of professionals as a whole was long and bloody, as represented most publicly by the teachers' strikes, but probably most significantly for her personal future in the arguments over GP budgets and over the relative powers of the judiciary. Welfare was guilty because of its connections with professionalism.

Third, welfare was guilty in Thatcher's eyes because of its association with local authority and, therefore, with the local state. For local authorities were themselves accused of inefficiency and incompetence as well as political and sometimes deliberate sabotage (viz the community charge). The 1980s for Thatcher were a running battle to bring local authorities to account.

And so, social welfare, like housing and education before it, became caught up in a broader battle arena that was essentially about state control and the nature of democracy and not about welfare at all. Who makes the decisions and where are they made? Does the elected representative sit in the town hall or in Westminster? What is the nature of that representation and how does it tally with strong state control, not even from Westminster, not even from the Cabinet, but increasingly in the late 1980s, from No. 10.

These three explanations do much to explain why social welfare, like other public services, was scapegoated, even rubbished, under Thatcher, and, therefore, ripe for change. But how was it that the application of free market principles became the dominant solution? There are at least four reasons for this.

The first is the obvious one that central government controlled the mechanisms for implementation (in this case legislation and the purse-strings) and could, therefore, choose the remedy. Indeed the late 1980s and early 1990s saw a vast legislative programme steered through parliament with only cursory attention to due consultative processes and sometimes paying heavily for this. (For example, the creation of the council tax was a reaction to a failed string of devices for controlling local authority spending from the centre, with the intention of making local authorities accountable to the funder/consumer.) Control of implementation mechanisms was accompanied by tactical manoeuvres involving leakages to the press (e.g. on the Chancellor's Autumn Statement), careful timing of publications (e.g. the Griffiths Review of Community Care (1988) and major precursor to the White Paper, *Caring for People* (1989) on the Royal Wedding Day), and the use of veiled threats (e.g. on the future of the Probation Service in the 1989 Green Paper, *Supervision and Punishment in the Community* (1990)).

Second, the ideological argument was reinforced, reinterpreted and sometimes replaced by a financial one. Where conflicts of value can be converted to conflicts of interest, or even better, blamed jointly on a third force, they become much easier to manage. And so the control of public expenditure, in itself a very real issue, became the mechanism for dealing with a conflict of ideology. The White Paper, *Caring for People* (1989), epitomises this: it can be read either as an ideological treatise or as a financial document.

Third, Thatcher's government, it seemed, was the only party in the 1980s to put forward techniques (as opposed to ideologies) by which public service organisations could be reformed. The promotion of Thatcher's ideology may have been distasteful to some in welfare, but few could dispute the value of the techniques of audit, unit accounting, evaluation on performance, and quality assurance. In a shared perception of the problems of cash-limiting and of then rationing public expenditure, these techniques made sense.

Yet on the back of these techniques could be constructed a whole set of market-induced solutions to controlling public expenditure (internal markets, opting out, competitive tendering, privatisation); a set of processes for filtering out conflict, such as procrastination (the government response to the Griffiths Review of Community Care) or reorganisation of elected bodies (as with the Probation Service and the Health Service); the deliberate upstaging of non-viable alternatives (such as electronic tagging in the Probation Service); the use of Green Papers as if they had the status of White Papers (as with the 1990 Green Paper on the Probation Service); the disaggregation of opposition by buying off interest groups (such as rises for teachers and university lecturers); and the making of direct deals with the consumer (as with school parent-governors).

The effect of all this, and the fourth explanation for the way in which free market solutions became received wisdom, is what has become known as Thatcher's control of the moral high ground. Stuart Hall (1983) describes how the language of the left and the centre were hijacked by Thatcherism to create a moral dimension to party politics that was unassailable. The Conservative party under Thatcher became the party of the family, of the inner city, of the community, sharing words but not necessarily meanings with the voters. For to Thatcherism the family was the personification of the unit of self-help, the building block of a community based on self-responsibility.

But the real success of Thatcher's control of the moral high ground lay in the identification of shifts in values with clear policy outcomes, such that notions of consumer choice were attached to the sale of council houses.

And so we begin to understand why a particular construction of the problems of welfare and the state become canvassed and become even received wisdom in many quarters. But what promoted that construction and that promotion? For criticisms about the viability, the success and the desirability of the post-war welfare state were emerging before Thatcher and before free market solutions became popularized in the UK. So what was that failure about, and why should free market solutions appear constructive in that situation?

There are broadly two explanations, or levels of explanation. The first sees long-term changes in the world economy which find specific expression in Thatcherism in the UK. Andrew Gamble (1988), for example, sees Thatcher and Reagan as responses to the breakdown of US economic supremacy and the authority of the social democratic state. He relates UK experience to world recession, and would now no doubt include within that the Eastern bloc economies. Gamble points to the failure of corporatist solutions to economic problems (i.e. state, business and trade unions working together) and to failures in political representation such that the ballot box no longer represents the views of the majority. For Gamble, issues of race, gender, public order and nationality are then not simply issues in themselves, but modes by which change in the role of state is achieved. What that means is that issues like apartheid in South Africa, like disability rights in the UK, like public order and nationality issues in the emergent Eastern bloc countries are attempts to create a new state order; not so much, in Gamble's view at least, the fag end of Thatcherism as the fag end of capitalism. In this scenario Thatcherism emerges not as an end in itself, but as a medium for hegemonic shift.

For Gamble then, the creation of the strong state is a necessary prerequisite for a free economy. In other words, a free market depends on being able to construct and maintain the conditions of relative freedom. This goes some way to explain the paradox of the promotion of a strong state that yet claims it is rolling back, as in Thatcherism. It explains also the conflict between central and local government with the centre at once backing off but reluctant to invest power in the local state (viz Griffiths 1988).

The second view, and one that finds popularity in our everyday explanations of an everyday world, is that the political trends of the 1980s can only be explained by Thatcherism (Jenkins 1987) or, in Riddell's (1989) view, by the presence of Thatcher herself. In this interpretation the whole debate is one about the managerial capacity of the state to manage. Solutions are, therefore, around reformation of the machinery of management or government, such as reform of the Civil Service and management of the Cabinet. In this view, managerial failure of the government to govern has arisen out of a breakdown of co-operation due mainly to the insurrectionist behaviour of the trade unions and the largely uncontrollable interests of big business. Resolution lies in reaffirming the control of the state, disempowering trade unions and bringing checks and balances into business interests within a broadly free market. The meteoric rise of the Audit Commission in the 1980s represents one such check.

Resolution lies also in the management of opposition in the form of other political parties by such means as altering local authority boundaries, reviewing tiers of local government, and dismembering sizeable and influential coalitions like the Greater London Council. Here, in other words, is a technician's view of politics.

Of course the value of competing explanations is in their potential for complementarity. Both the long-term and the technical explanation are different levels of analysis of the same set of events. Of course there is a global level of explanation for why Thatcherism not only took off in Britain, but assumed such apparent world-wide credibility. And of course there is a back door explanation that is about the nuts and bolts of managing individual and pressure group power struggles.

Implications for public service managers

There are at least three implications here for public service managers. First, policy about public service is not only, or even necessarily primarily interested in public service. It may be designed to serve political interests. This is not a cynical view either of social policy or of government. It is simply a recognition that politics is intrinsic to managing in public service, not a bolted on extra.

Second, public policy has complex objectives. It is both value driven and resource driven (as well as reflecting needs). Issues of ideology and issues of resourcing are not alternative sets of objectives. They may compete, but both are central.

Third, public policy is part of a much broader arena which takes in the relationship between the individual and the state and the conditions for representation of that individual to the state and vice versa. It is not sufficient, for example, to consider services for the elderly, people with disabilities, or children at risk, without considering the kind of society and structures that create vulnerable groups within it, or the nature of any responsibility that society may have towards them.

ECONOMIC TRENDS

For managers in public service agencies, resource constraints assumed increasing significance throughout the 1980s. Where, for example, finance and treasurers' sections in local authority departments existed in the 1960s and even to some extent in the 1970s, in order to service operations, in the 1980s they increasingly dominated them. The creation of the delegated/ designated budget holder, the specification of contracts and intended outcomes and renewed emphasis on quality control were all features of a local economy which took money much more seriously.

Why? Where did the pressure come from to account for financial activities? Why have bodies like CIPFA and the Audit Commission assumed such prominence in local authority activities?

There are broadly two sets of explanations for the behaviour of the UK economy in the 1980s. Again, they are macro and micro, long-term and short-term.

The long-term theory comes in various forms. The first, drawing on Kuhn's (1970) notion of 'paradigm', or Gramsci's (1988) 'hegemony', or Foucault's (1986) 'discourse' relates world recession to periodisation in historical terms, and to regionalisation in geographic terms. It says that a whole era, with its whole political and economic philosophy, is drawing to a close; an era based on Western supremacy, on national economic boundaries and on urbanisation. It points to new economic boundaries, such as the EC or the Third World. In terms of economic theory this closure is marked by the collapse of Keynesian and monetarist theories alike, by brief flirtations with neo-classical economies and by the reopening of the Eastern bloc countries. Bell (1974), in another version of the same theory, talks about the managerial revolution and the rise of the service sector over the production sector. Even the advertising world reflects changes in the labour market, in production and consumption patterns with enhanced sectorisation and fudged class boundaries. For Gamble (1988), the changes are inescapably attached to the decline in supremacy of the United States and with it the capitulation of Fordism: that model associated with factories, with urban sites, with the division of labour and the whole notion of industrialism.

In this view, Thatcher's continual hankering after expansion of a declining manufacturing base had to be a lost cause. Decentralisation of industry and the control of public expenditure were simply devices to extend the 'product life' of an economy in transit. That transition is to a service economy in the UK based on a world market, not of manufacture, but of financial services and product aggregation.

In contrast the short-term or 'blip' theory suggests that the broadly erratic pattern of the economy is related to the competence of government to govern and the range of available instruments to enforce economic restrictions. Significant here is investment in and subsequent failure of the planning model of the 1960s and 1970s, whereby volume planning and specification of resources resulted in inflexible service provision. Attempts to address this inflexibility by one-off interventions only served to create unintended consequences, the classic example of which was the perverse incentive identified by the Audit Commission Report on Community Care, whereby elderly persons were encouraged to enter expensive residential care at cost to the taxpayer. As each instrument for adjusting the economy developed defects through the domino effect, it was abandoned. This included price constraint, wage restraint, curbs on consumer spending and credit restrictions until, under Nigel Lawson, the very blunt instrument of interests rates was regarded as the only effective weapon against what was for Thatcher the singular enemy of inflation.

The problem was perceived by public services as a constraint on public expenditure. This meant first of all cash-limiting public expenditure. First attempts at this (such as the Social Fund) were spectacular in their failure. Once cash-limited, the debate then centred around the rationing of services, and a whole new set of indicators was established to facilitate this, based on something the Treasury and the Audit Commission called 'value for money' and 'the 3Es' (economy, efficiency, effectiveness). The debate moved away from one about imputs to one about outputs. Services were asked to state their objectives and measure effectiveness against them. Entrepreneurial management was coined, fostered by the outstandingly popular Peters and Waterman publication (1982), an action-packed collection on the rhetoric of innovation, which owed little to management theory but undoubtedly suited the philosophy of the day.

Meanwhile, continuing failure to stem public expenditure, combined with what presented to the Thatcher government as the recalcitrant behaviour of some Labour councils in spite of rate-capping and tapering, meant that some groups had to be taken out of coverage altogether, notably the 16–18-year-olds who became dependent again upon parental income. In this scenario, the ill-fated community charge, begun no doubt as a response to an inequitable rating system, gathered momentum as a mechanism for forcing not the government, but consumers of services themselves to control the expenditure of local authorities.

Reducing spending was complemented by mechanisms designed to ring-fence money (such as specific grants for the elderly, children and management development in Social Services). In addition, direct grants to voluntary organisations (such as the NSPCC National Training Centre construction), and pump priming of independent organisations (such as NACRO) offered an early backdoor solution to controlling spending by creating false competition in the market place of welfare, later extended to require percentage spending in the independent sector (for example in the Community Care Special Transitional Grant).

Both macro and micro explanations of the economy are of value to the manager. At one level it is becoming increasingly obvious that the world is the unit of the new economy, and the new unit of recession. The simple correlation between the New York, Tokyo and London Stock Exchanges points that up daily. It is, however, very difficult to operate in such a large context, and so managers find themselves operating at levels of explanation at which they can themselves intervene. That means operating less at the level of the EC, even at the level of government and more at the level of local political parties and local budget. We know that to criticise the Chancellor is to shoot the messenger, but we cannot handle the message or where it is coming from.

The effect is to create a contradiction between measures designed to promote the broad conditions under which resurgence of the economy can take place, and those designed to cut out risk and guarantee certainty.

What that means in practice both for central government and local authorities is the push towards an accountant's rather than an economist's view of welfare; an obsession with budget and public expenditure. Health, Social Services and Social Security, for example, could only be contained within separate budget heads where spending and accountability for spending could be contained by cut back on joint or peripheral responsibilities or controlled with joint commissioning contracts. In this view, Griffiths' view of a community care agency that would draw together departmental figurations under one set of responsibilities was at once visionary and devastating to a government committed to controlling public expenditure.

Implications for public service managers

There are lessons once again here for managers in public service agencies. First, the availability of money for public service provision broadly correlates with levels of economic growth and not with levels of identified need. Of course, ideological or pragmatic factors may influence decisions to invest in personal social services, such as education and health in the 1948 Education Act and 1946 Health Services Act, but not normally in care of what may be regarded as a permanently dependent population (e.g. the elderly and people with severe handicaps). The creation of an open-ended budget in health welfare has been a function not of welfare itself, or of ideology, but primarily of economic boom which allowed the popularisation of a welfare philosophy.

Two implications follow for care service managers. The health of the economy is of permanent concern, and the relationship between economies and ideology is complex, but nonetheless central to under-standing and predicting levels of public provision.

Second, pressure to measure outputs and effectiveness is a trend in response to the failure of the planning model, and needs to be viewed as such.

Third, in an uncertain world, explanations tend to focus on the here and now and the close to home. That the Director of Social Services, the Chair of Committee, the Chancellor, the Prime Minister, the level of interest rates, the community charge are at fault, are all such explanations. They are in fact contributions to an explanation, the complexity of which tends to paralyse action. This is no reason for not seeking to understanding the complexity, nor for intervening at the everyday level.

The final point is that in times of economic stress, it is a buyer's market. This may suggest that the rise of consumerism in the market place, in welfare in particular and in the economy in general, may have less to do with human rights than the personal income levels of some sectors. It is important not to confuse the two.

SOCIAL STRUCTURE

How significant are the changes which have taken place in the social structure in the UK in recent decades? Moreover, are they permanent? These questions are at the root of managerial responses to public service. If, for example, family breakdown and reconstitution is to be an ongoing feature of the social structure, what does that mean for the care of those indirectly or directly affected by it, such as children and grandparents? If, for example, women are to be drawn back into paid labour, what does that mean for policies dependent upon their presence in the home, such as community care? For the form services take, and indeed their selection of target groups, need to be both responsive to and predictive of broad social trends.

The answer is that there are broadly two interpretations of the significance and permanence of those trends, and that there are also broadly two explanations for them.

But first of all what do we mean by social structure and what changes are regarded as taking place? The most significant changes for health and social care services managers are in the three areas of social divisions, the family and employment patterns. Employment patterns will be given special attention later in this chapter under the heading of Technology.

Looking then at social divisions, the first major change is in the primary division of social class. Within social class at least four changes can be identified. First the single pre-eminence of class as the primary source of social division appears to be wavering. Of course this view is controversial. Ever since the term 'managerial revolution' (Bell 1974) was coined and since the research of Goldthorpe *et al.* (1968) was popularised, there have been those who have pointed to the supposed breakdown in the construction of social class in post-war Britain, and with it, the supposed breakdown in a Marxist conception of the universe. This is not that sort of argument. In contrast, there have been those who have argued that such changes as are occurring to the class structure are simply in terms of its redefinition and reconstruction. In other words, that inequality simply takes on different forms within a redefined class structure. Such theorists explain, for instance, the place of women and black persons within the labour force with reference to class divisions. This is not that sort of argument either.

It is not, in other words, an either/or argument. It simply points up that whilst inequalities most certainly remain, and for some groups at least are enhanced (viz the new 'underclass'), life chances are increasingly cumulatively determined. Most certainly, to be born with a silver spoon in one's mouth still and absolutely overwhelming determines one's chances of reaching the Bench. But to be born black and to be born a woman is to guarantee at least equivalent lack of privilege. That is not to argue that the significance of class division is waning. It is to argue rather that social divisions in themselves are becoming more complex, and of more rather than less significance overall in determining life chances.

Second, within the social division of class, the working-class element is changing most significantly. It is first of all diversifying and decomposing. Doreen Massey (1988) points to a decline in traditional manual workers (60 per cent of the working population in 1961 compared to 50 per cent in 1981), often mistakenly referred to as a shrinkage in the population of the working class (and often used to explain the decline in the Labour vote in the 1980s). Kendrick *et al.* argue a shift instead towards employment in service industries, much of which is unskilled and non-manual and arguably still working class. It is suggested that these changes are resulting in a working class divided by those in full-time, often traditional or new service industries, from those in part-time, temporary and often self-employed work or dependent on state benefits. The latter are increasingly being referred to as an 'underclass'. Also, the working class is becoming feminised. Catherine Hakim (1980) reveals that the new flexible workforce, identified by her as part-time, temporary or self-employed, is overwhelmingly female. Suzanne King (1986) adds that temporary workers are most likely to be female, married and older or younger rather than middle-aged.

For Peter Saunders (1989) and Gordon Marshall *et al.* (1988), the changes that are occurring in class divisions are most extreme at the points of internal class boundaries. Looking at class from the point of view of consumption patterns, Marshall argues that state intervention in housing, health and education has broken down traditional class boundaries, the most significant of these being home ownership. For him it is not that embougeoisement of the working class (as defined by Goldthorpe *et al.* 1968) has taken place, but that relations between the state and the market have been changed, one outcome of which has been a confusion over how class boundaries can be defined. Any intended shift to private health and private education should not, in his view, be confused with changes in class, and above all, not be confused with changes in voting behaviour. Certainly participation in alternative forms of social education may be expected to influence votes in the long term, but consumer behaviour is not in itself to be regarded as evidence of shifts in political affiliation. Meanwhile for Saunders, the disaggregation of defined class boundaries leads him to talk not of class but of groups distinguished by consumption patterns. In other words, of consumption cleavages or market segments.

Finally, class divisions are themselves being complicated by other forms of social division, notably race and gender. Certainly equal opportunities and race relations legislation has not as yet resulted in wide acceptance of women and black people in high-status jobs, but that is arguably not a function of class. Indeed patriarchal explanations of women's position in society point to the persistence of women in high status positions long before current history, and seeks an explanation for their apparent invisibility in historical accounts not simply in terms of class position but in terms of gender inequality.

Moving on now to look at changes in family and household structures and behaviours, Halsey (1989) summarises a number of trends:

- more women, especially married women, in employment;
- less childbirth, but more illegitimate childbirth;
- more divorce and remarriage and more one-person households;
- more men economically inactive, whether as unemployed, retired or drawn into the domestic economy;
- more men and women in adult education;
- more children in extended schooling;
- a population with higher formal qualifications.

The assumption behind this shift is one of a family which can cope and which must cope with its elderly, its children and its handicapped, an assumption which is problematic given statistics on the breakdown and reconstitution of families and on the changing role of women as employees rather than, or as well as, primary carers.

The separation of health services into purchasers and providers and the stimulation of a private sector can be regarded as responses to overdemand on rationed services.

Of equal significance for providers is the ways in which these changes in family roles and responsibilities arise out of, and in themselves stimulate, the breakdown of traditional perceptions and behaviours in and around family relationships and behaviours. The breakdown and reconstitution of the family, the reintegration of women into the workforce and the discharge of men from it raise uncertainties about the traditional locus and, therefore, meaning of gender relations. Notions of childhood, adulthood, work, leisure and learning similarly take on new meanings and new uncertainties in a way that can no longer be stereotyped into crude explanations like those of the generation gap or women's liberation.

In this way the whole construction of the family as the building block of community and thus of state is called into question as it diversifies, destabilises and, above all, changes in meaning due to the very participation of its members.

There are broadly two explanations for these changes in social structure. One focuses on the long-term historical, geographical and demographic moves which came together in the 1980s to form nothing less than a paradigm shift. For Peter Hall (1988) this new phase of development is the fifth Kondratieff, whose cause is identified by Christopher Freeman (1982) as located in the communication revolution arising out of the technology of the computer chip. For Halsey (1989), it is changes in the labour market which herald 'a whole new phase of economic and social transformation'. And increasingly for the Thatcher government it was the perceived demographic time bomb of an increased elderly and a reduced youth population which forced the pace, a timebomb later challenged (Hills 1993). But whether explanations are located in technological, economic or demographic determinism (and probably in truth in all three), the consensus is that these changes in the social structure are significant, dramatic even, and if not permanent, most certainly long-term.

In contrast, an alternative set of explanations for changes in the social structure focuses on what are perceived as incremental events which gradually begin to shape Britain in a certain direction, but which are mistakenly perceived in dramatic terms. Thus the oil crisis of 1974 and the policies of the Thatcher government, aggressive industrial relations and consumer preference begin to impact upon family life, but family life in turn takes and shapes economic and political patterns in the workplace and in government. In a view traditionally associated with Weber, it is the social structure that determines what goes on in the workplace and not vice versa.

The reality probably lies somewhere between both sets of explanation. Halsey, whilst he sees a paradigm shift in process, sees the trigger to that in the later 1970s oil crisis: not simply an evolutionary but also a jump-start view of history.

Implications for public service managers

First, health and welfare services have a political responsibility to respond to pressures of change in social structure and tend to do so in a time warp. Such services have a social responsibility to be proactive as well as reactive in this climate, and, therefore, to create services and service organisations which are predictive of future trends. Care service managers operate at the sharp end of this interface between two time scales and two sets of responsibilities for users and politicians here and now and in the future.

Second, some of the policy initiatives promoted by the Thatcher administration were in conflict with social trends and most especially with those trends that indicated changes in the family and in female employment patterns. Care in the Community policies were one example of this.

Third, the potential for the creation of an underclass arising out of the redefinition of the public and private responsibilities and fragmentation/ polarisation of traditional social class grouping must be of serious concern to those whose business is the service of vulnerable groups.

Fourth, race and gender issues in employment are not simply an outcome of political preferences or fashion, but represent major and long-term changes in social relations in the UK and are, therefore, integral to developing services for the 1990s.

Finally, the locus and nature of social care interventions is likely to change as family roles and responsibilities change. New gender patterns, cultural variation, women in work and new patterns of child rearing will make new and enhanced skill and resource demands on both practitioners and managers.

TECHNOLOGY

The computer revolution, the service economy and the managerial revolution are all terms that try to capture different aspects of the changing technology of work in the last decades of the twentieth century. What do these terms mean, and what significance, if any, do they have for managers designing, commissioning and delivering services in the 1990s? Significant changes in the content of work, the construction of the labour force and the design of work processes are addressed under the following headings:

- what is the nature of the work done?
- who does the work?
- where does the work take place?
- how is work organised?

Again, competing explanations are given for these changes and messages drawn out for public services managers.

What is the nature of the work?

Looking first at what work is done, a well-publicised decline in manufacturing jobs in the economy as a whole (36 per cent in 1961 compared with 28 per cent in 1981 according to Massey 1988) is associated, for some with a massive shift into the post-industrial service, or tertiary, economy (Clark 1940). For Richard Walker (1988) the shift is not so large nor so dramatic. Distinguishing a service from a manufacturing economy as one defined by its outputs or products rather than by its takeover force or employment patterns, he queries the categorisation that places some jobs in the service sector. In particular he argues that a rapid increase in public sector and professional services in the last twenty years have been confused with an expansion in the service sector. Certainly, taking workforce size as an indicator suggests that the larger local authorities in the 1980s competed for size with the top ten blue chip companies in the UK.

Who does the work?

Looking at who does the work, new trends emerge. The work is increasingly taken on by a flexible work force, typically part-time, self-employed or temporary (Hakim 1987). It is increasingly taken on by women (King 1986). In other words 'the rapid fall in full-time employment for men in the eighties masked a subtler increase in part-time working for women (King 1986). It is increasingly professional and managerial in content. In general terms then, skilled manual work is giving way to unskilled manual work and to high-status professional and managerial jobs. The reconstruction of the workforce has been described by Leadbeater (1989) in four segments; core, peripheral, short-term unemployed and long-term unemployed. Handy (1994) makes a much sharper distinction between those working inside organisations and those who move in and out of them.

Where does the work take place?

At one level there is continuing decline in regional and structural industries, such as in coal, steel and shipbuilding. Combined with this is the deindustrialisation of the cities, the effects of which are more dramatic and more sudden, in the North West and the West Midlands where relative affluence has, in working-class terms, turned to poverty.

At another level potentially regenerative processes are taking place. Massey (1984) points to the increasing centrality of London. In 1977, 300 of the top 350 UK firms were headed by managerial capacity in the capital. This is in distinct contrast to production, which appears to be firmly regionalised with an increasing tendency to decentralise and relocate outside London to match shifting cheap labour availability and labour shortages in the capital. Local trading estates are springing up to take advantage of the new flexible workforce. Finally, there is a growth in specialist and professional services increasingly located in what Massey calls the 'British Sunbelt' of Bristol, Southampton and Cambridge.

How is work organised?

Three new features emerge. First managerialism and labour or production are increasingly separated both in function and geography, typically with regionalised, even localised production units and a centralised managerial headquarters in London. Improved communication, both in terms of personal transport and transfer of information, are regarded as responsible for this trend, together with regional house prices and the increasing breakdown of national pay bargaining.

Second, some experts, usually professionals, are increasingly being bought in by firms on an occasional or contract basis rather than employed by them. Such experts may or may not be geographically located near their clients (viz Massey's Sunbelt). Mintzberg (1983) refers to these experts as 'technicians', they may be accountants, information technology staff or increasingly, management consultants.

This helps to explain the third emerging feature of work organisation, which is the apparent contradiction in the rise of very large or very small firms. At one level there is the multi-national conglomerate, such as Storehouse, which characterised the early 1980s, only to collapse by the end of the decade. At another there is the very small, very new firm, often simply a handful of professionals and support staff operating in a very clearly defined market niche.

The effect of these three features of work organisation in combination is to produce potentially quite different work structures to those to which we have traditionally become accustomed, namely those of the factory and the city. The separation of the management and production processes has traditionally brought with it line hierarchy. This hierarchy is now extended and dispersed by geographical distance and dominated by the centrality of a headquarters office leading to problems of control between centre and periphery. The potential exclusion of certain sorts of permanent expertise from the firm due to the decanting of some professionals may lead to short-term efficiency and leanness but can mean a loss of wisdom and, often more significantly, potential confrontation between the remaining two major interest groups of managers and production workers. Finally, the change in size of companies leads on the one hand to small-batch, customer-conscious, craft-made production, and on the other to uniformity and standardisation of design and production. Either way it tends to lead to instability of firms and constant restructuring although in practice large firms are often conglomerates of small firms and small-batch production. This instability is characterised by the dramatic changes in fortune of Sock Shop and Knickerbox in the niche markets, and by the creation and recreation of trusts and joint commissioning agencies in order to achieve vertical integration and meet consumption requirements in the Health Service.

Once again there are two levels of explanation for these changes. Freeman (1982) and Massey (1984) point to long-run processes of change which are geographical and economic in character, and talk about changes in the construction and geography of the labour force. Kendrick *et al.* agree, seeing the shift as part of a long-term historical trend from extractive (agricultural) to productive (manufacturing) and finally to service industries.

For others, such as Ken Mayhew (1988), the changes are much more associated with short-term explanations such as the dynamic of government's relationship with industry. His view is supported by the 1985 White Paper, *Employment: The Challenge for the Nation* which regarded high unemployment as due to lack of flexibility in the labour market combined with 'wage pushfulness' and over-rigidity. Solutions in this view are, therefore, about 'freeing the market at the bottom end', by the reform of collective bargaining and by training and mobility policies.

Implications for public services managers

First, the obsession with the restructuring of large care service bureaucracies in the 1980s can be seen as a mirror image of changes that are taking place in the disintegration and reconstruction of firms in the market place.

Second, the rise of managerialism and the potential expulsion of some technical experts and professionals from large bureaucracies into private practices is part of a larger trend, and impacts on the nature of the organisation as a whole.

Third, the location of care service organisations and their concerns might be expected to shift with the geographical relocation of industry. This might be particularly true of city locations and inner-city concerns.

Fourth, the trend towards the creation of individual service responses to customers in care services in the form of care packages might be regarded as part of a wider move towards service management, small-batch production and consumerism.

Finally, public service reforms can be intepreted at two levels. For example, at one level the health service reforms can be seen as one of a series of vehicles for the implementation of transformational change from services which are driven by providers, by professionals and by technology to those chosen by communities. In this view the shift from acute to primary and community care can be interpreted as a shift from product to consumer orientation, or, using a community development model, to consumer driven product development. At another level they are simply technical changes required to manage the market. It remains to be seen whether or not provider, purchaser and regulator mergers in the 1990s will, given their prevalence, assume transformational significance overall. If so, we might expect that those commenced for reasons of politics, or vertical integration, or cost saving will not simply recycle existing products but, taking the community as their customer, will demand and will create new packages of care.

REFERENCES

Bell, D. (1974), *The Coming of Post-industrial Society,* New York: Basic Books

Clark, C. (1940), *The Conditions of Economic Progress*, London: Macmillan

D.H. and D.S.S. (1989), *Caring for People, Community care in the next decade and beyond*, London: HMSO

Foucault, M. (1986), *Foucault Reader*, Rabinow, P. (ed), London: Penguin

Freeman, C. (1982), *Technology, Policy and Economic Performance: Lessons from Japan.*

Gamble, A. (1988), *The Free Economy and the Strong State: Politics of Thatcherism*, Basingstoke: Macmillan

Goldthorpe, J.H. *et al.* (1968), *The Affluent Worker: Industrial Attitudes and Behaviour*, Cambridge: Cambridge University Press

Gramsci, A. (1988), *A Gramsci Reader*, Forgacs, D. (ed), Hoare, Q. (translation), London: Lawrence and Wishart Ltd

Griffiths, R. (1988), *Community Care: agenda for action*, London: HMSO

Hakim, C. (1980) Census reports as documentaty evidence: the census commentaries 1801–1951, *Sociological Review*, vol. 28, No. 3, August

Hall, P. (1988), The geography of the fifth Kondratieff, in Massey and Allen (eds) *Uneven Redevelopment, Cities and Regions in Transition: A Reader*, London: Hodder and Stoughton in association with OU Press

Hall, S. (1983), *Politics of Thatcherism*, London: Lawrence and Wishart Ltd

Halsey, A.H. (1989), Social trends since World War II, in McDowell, L., Scarre, P. and Hamnett, C. (eds), *Divided Nation, Social and Cultural Change in Britain: A Reader*, London: Hodder and Stoughton in association with OU Press

Handy, C. (1994), *The empty raincoat: making sense of the future*, London: Hutchinson

Hills, J. (1993), *The Future of Welfare: a guide to the debate*, York: Joseph Rowntree Foundation

Home Office (1990), *Supervision and Punishment in the Community: a Framework For Action (Cmnd 966)* London: HMSO

Jenkins, P. (1987), *Mrs Thatcher's Revolution: Ending of the Socialist Era*, London: Jonathan Cape

King, S. (1988), The changing social structure in Massey and Allen (eds) *Uneven Redevelopment, Cities and Regions in Transition: A Reader*, London: Hodder and Stoughton in association with OU Press

Kuhn, T.S. (1970), *The Structure of Scientific Revolutions*, Chicago: University of Chicago Press

Leadbeater, C. (1989) In the land of the dispossessed in McDowell, L., Scarre, P. and Hamnett, C. (eds) D*ivided Nation; Social And Cultural Change in Britain*, London: Hodder and Stoughton in association with OU Press

Marshall, G. (1988), *Social Class in Modern Britain*, London: Hutchinson

Massey, D. (1984), *Spatial divisions of labour: social structures and the geography of production*, London: Macmillan

Mintzberg, H (1983), *Structure in Fives: Designing Effective Organisations*, Englewood Cliffs, NJ: Prentice-Hall

Mishra, R. (1984), *The Welfare State in Crisis*, Brighton: Harvester-Wheatsheaf

Peters, T.J. and Waterman, R.H. (1982), *In Search of Excellence*, New York: Harper and Row

Riddell, P. (1989), *Thatcher Decade*, Oxford: Blackwell

Saunders, P. (1989), Beyond housing classes: the sociological significance of private property rights in means of consumption in McDowell, L., Sarre, P. and Hamnett, C. (eds) *Divided Nation, Social and Cultural Change in Britain,* London: Hodder and Stoughton

UK Government White Paper (1985), *Employment: The Challenge for the Nation*, CMND 94764, London: HMSO

CHAPTER THREE

The heritage of care services: their role and function

SUMMARY

To understand how and why management in public service agencies works or does not work is not simply to see it as a response to the pressures of the external environment (chapter 2), but as part of a heritage. That heritage has traditionally been part of the construction of expectations and body of knowledge owned by professional practitioners. It is, however, not only theirs. Constructing forms of management appropriate to care service agencies must include valuing and taking on that aspect of the professional heritage. The emergence of managerialism has, it seems, all too often been at the expense of the professional. Sharing an understanding of heritage, and of the values which underpin it, is one way of bringing managers and professionals together, a way already acknowledged by those professionals turned managers.

In an attempt to do just that, this chapter looks at the development of services in one care setting – in this case children – as a model for comparison with others. It argues that the development of services are beset with fundamental paradoxes or contradictions which are now being passed on from the professional to the manager for resolution. Those contradictions are not open to resolution, but represent fundamental differences of interests and of values. This chapter considers three of them and argues for a form of managerialism which understands the nature of these dilemmas and seeks to manage with them, not in spite of them.

- How are the needs of the user to be balanced against those of the family, the community and ultimately the state?
- What is the role of the family *vis à vis* care services? Carer? Controller? Or client?

- Who is (or in what balance) ultimately responsible for services? User? Professional? Manager? Carer? Politician? And what is the nature of their authority over those services?

THE NEEDS OF THE USER

Using child-care services as a model for other services we find that the concept of the child as a user of services is of very recent origin. Indeed before the Victorian era, childhood as such did not exist. Pre-Victorian painting represents children as infants or as mini-adults. Infancy was modelled on the infant Jesus and ended abruptly at the age of seven, the age of responsibility for mortal sin.

In legislation, children appear first as heirs in property suits, when they were treated as the property of the father; or as offenders and threats to public order, when they were treated the same as adult offenders. From the beginning, then, children gave rise to public concern not in their own right as children but as in need of the protection or control of others. Children did not have rights because they were the property and hence the responsibility of the father, or failing that, the state. The theory of human rights subsequently overlaid but did not replace this fundamental relationship of unequal power which runs right through the provision of service from 1800.

Indeed state intervention on any scale in the role of children did not occur until the family itself was taken up by the state as a public burden. At this point some children were identified as social problems. This began to happen with the 1833 Factory Act which limited the hours worked by women and children and therefore separated them from men as less productive. With the 1870 Education Act children moved away from being economic assets to the family and became private joys and/or private burdens. The reaction to the scandal of baby-farming represented a wave of protection towards children, resulting in more legislation.

At this point we see the beginnings of a Victorian theory about the origins of problem children: they are either depraved or deprived. Along with the theory came a set of solutions. Depraved children were segregated into reform schools or industrial schools, or, lest the transmission of evil prove too risky, shipped off to the new commonwealth. Deprived children were rescued by benevolent individuals or by God and placed in foster care (boarded out) or residential care. The distinction serves that of Victorian society at large, where degeneracy is seen as located in the idle working classes and urban

31

centres, virtue is a product of gentle breeding and/or hard work; and where out of sight is out of mind. To this notion we owe the present identification of a 'hard core' seen as idle and unrehabilitative, and the creation of two separate systems for treatment and for punishment.

By 1900 we already have a justification for intervention in certain situations based on a certain 'theory', and childrens' services being delivered in a relatively coherent and standardised way that was to dominate the next century.

The major threat to that domination comes after the Second World War with a new theory: John Bowlby's (1970) identification of maternal deprivation as the major cause of creating problem children. Children were the focus of the new post-war drive and its greatest potential resource. They must be healthy, educated and, above all, bonded with natural parents.

The war period illustrates more than any other how services for children exist not only for the benefit of those children, but to serve the needs, aspirations and ideals of the wider community and society in which they operate. The reverse side of that is how far services exist to penalise or stigmatise those families and those individuals who do not go along with this image.

Because children are traditionally seen as inarticulate, others can assume that they know best. Children's dependence and lack of franchise mean they are particularly vulnerable to stereotyping, and this occurs of course in the notion of the depraved and the deprived child. Such rigid stereotyping makes it difficult to articulate children's rights successfully. Similarly, it leaves them open to the construction of social problems, potentially without their consent or contribution. The evidence is that children probably see their problems quite differently from the public, the media or their social workers, as shown in the dialogue on child sexual abuse.

THE ROLE OF THE FAMILY

The development of child-care services continues to demonstrate the ways in which public services pick up piecemeal on ongoing social dilemmas, in this case on the role of the family. What we have already by the 1870s–1890s is the establishment of certain sorts of families as in need of special provision, and crucially not others. The common denominator in this stereotyping process is poverty.

With the Victorians, the kind of care provided for children takes on a particular dimension: it becomes substitute family care. If the large Victorian institutions seem distanced from our current nuclear relationships, they were built in fact very much along Victorian family lines. Often benevolent in origin, they were designed to mop up the increasing mass of dislocated and economically unsound individuals displaced by the break-up of the extended family due to urban concentration and industrial development. Later institutional forms clarified the patriarchal pattern, with Scattered Homes, for example, operating as small units on a large site. We have here the beginning of the process of breaking up large caring units into smaller family groups, which reaches its peak with the post-war Family Group Homes.

Services for children created after the war represent the nation's investment in its own future. It has been argued that the creation of the welfare state, with the Beveridge package of health services, unemployment and sickness insurance, education and children's services, represented a consensus on the provision of welfare, and with it, equality. An alternative view is that the welfare state was the price paid to buy off working-class militancy, with unemployed patriots unable to find work and families homeless. In either interpretation the family as a building block of society was central to the revitalisation of the economy and the new welfare state.

The notion of the family, based on marriage, monogamy, joint child rearing and economic dependency, had come under serious threat in the war years. In the absence of their menfolk some women had taken on war work, male occupations, even other relationships, and a few had become economically independent. The war took its toll in terms of broken and bereaved families. Over 1,300,000 women and children had been evacuated from urban centres, with consequent effects on home and community. There were stories of the urban deprivation of children.

The solution to these sorts of problems was to promote a return to family life, a solution not unfamiliar (though less successful) in the early 1980s under Thatcher. Pathe News and newspaper reports of the period appealed to the 'nation's conscience' and women were asked to return to the home for the protection of their husbands and children. Magazines which previously extolled the virtues of convenience foods now pictured the busy housewife at home in her new kitchen creating time-consuming meals for her family.

And the nation responded. It responded by demands for housing of better quality and location. It responded by women giving up their jobs to men and above all, it responded with the baby boom of 1946-48. But this was no 'return' to family life. It was the making of a different kind of family. Gone were the days of servants. The working classes were literally on the move. The weekend was invented. Holiday camps were opened. The Labour Movement was mobilised.

The new family was nuclear, that is, it comprised parents and children with no extended relatives. It was a particular kind of family – an ideal family – which was picked up and institutionalised in the Beveridge proposals and which has confused child welfare ever since. It had five characteristics:

- It assumed female dependency on male income. Thus female benefits were marginalised and women drew off their partner's insurance.
- It assumed a special relationship between mother and children from which the father was excluded. Family Allowances for example, were to be paid to the woman, assuming she could be trusted not to divert resources from her own children.
- It assumed that men were the breadwinners and, therefore, that women's earnings were marginal ('pin money').
- It placed an obligation on family members to care for each other. The unit of the household was created as a unit of joint income and joint consumption.
- Above all, it assumed that everybody lived in families.

Subsequent services for health, housing, education, social security and welfare built on this ideal family model of a man working with a wife and dependent children at home. Services were, therefore, developed for those essential functions regarded by most as beyond the normal competency of most families. So while health and education services became national resource provisions, housing and welfare services remained open to individual and local demand/provision.

Where special services were developed they were only for families deviating from the ideal. It still remains much easier to live as a member of a certain kind of family, both economically and socially, than as an individual or as a member of a 'deviant' family, such as a gay couple. Stigmatisation of certain groups helped to ration the use of services.

Contradictions about the nature and function of the family became stylised with Beveridge and again with Thatcher into a particular kind of ideal family, at some variance with reality. Because the family is responsible for socialising the child into social order, welfare treads a very fine line. If it intervenes too much it destroys family responsibility; if it intervenes too little it risks the emergency of deviant and less controllable lifestyles into majority practice.

The nature of substitute care reflects this tightrope with swings between natural and substitute parenting. At present the trend is towards permanent placement of the child in the new family, towards parental rights and arguably towards childrens' rights, trends perhaps at variance with the demographic trends supporting less permanent and more flexible relationships.

WHO IS RESPONSIBLE FOR SERVICES?

As already identified, in law fathers were identified as responsible for, indeed owners of their children. This masked problems experienced by children. Child abuse, for example, certainly occurred. Records of abuse and infanticide abound both in mythology and literature from Hansel and Gretel to *The Water Babies*. But not until 1879 did the state intervene to protect children against cruelty: 75 years after legislation against cruelty to animals. Because this intervention was legalistic, it at once set up a heritage of adversarial confrontation between parent, child and state, and confounded subsequent interventions based on human rights (Parton 1985).

When state intervention did come it was arbitrary; the child care services found its origins in the Poor Law rather than in services specially designed for children. By 1908 there were 69,080 children in the workhouse with only 8,659 boarded out.

In the Victorian period poverty and distress were considered very much the fault of the individual, and their solution depended upon the moral character of that individual (deprived or depraved). State provision was supplemented by private benefaction.

The Poor Law was not abolished until 1948 when Children's Departments were set up within local authorities. The stigma of the Poor Law attached itself to the Children's Department and subsequently to Social Services Departments, a stigma reinforced by other agencies' attitudes, most notably the Health Service, which persists to the present day.

It was the creation of Children's Departments and with it the creation of Children's Officers, that, more than anything else changed the nature of the responsibility of the state to children within its care. It was this which led to the growth of bureaucracy and professionalism.

The creation of a local rather than a central government bureaucracy for children's services had a major impact on the identification and treatment of children with problems. First it compartmentalised their problems. In a period of economic expansion departmentalism could encourage specialisation. Against a backcloth of cuts it would enforce inherent competition between services for the same group of users. Education, housing, welfare and children's departments were all in competition for resources.

Second, the creation of a local committee made up of locally elected representatives and serviced by Children's Officers brought into sharp relief the contradiction in needing to provide special services for special children and the need to protect and serve the interests, including the financial interests, of the wider community.

Finally, the character of bureaucracy is such (see chapter 4) that it generated its own work, its own pace and its own solutions. Services for children became increasingly services organised in ways efficient for the organisation rather than effective for children. Staff shifts, central ordering of supplies, and so on are examples of this process.

The creation of Children's Officers led to the the professionalisation of Child Care Officers, and subsequently of social workers. A body of knowledge was quickly established, with a period of induction training increasingly required. That body of knowledge was based on a medical model which was firmly professional in intent (Friedson 1975).

Initially the body of knowledge was based on psychology, a paramedical subject imported from Europe and the United States in the 1950s along with television and washing machines. It was Freudian psychology that fell in particularly well with the new profession. Psychodynamic in approach, it stressed the value of early nurture and intervention in therapeutic form. Certain sorts of behaviour could be labelled as problematic and symptomatic of deeper distress.

Social problems it seemed, had causes, could be diagnosed, and could, therefore, be treated. It was simply a matter of understanding them better by a process of analysis and deduction. One result was that social problems were atomised and fragmented into individual problems. Children with problems became problem children and families with multiple problems became, in the jargon, 'problem families'. Social problems were simply collective versions of individual problems.

With the arrival of the 1960s, sociology began to take over from psychology as the main influence on the new profession. Many of its new recruits were themselves products of a first generation higher education system, and, not surprisingly, saw 'clients' like themselves, trapped by their social circumstances rather than by their own pathology.

The decade therefore saw the emergence of a series of social problems, many reflecting anxiety about the permissiveness of youth in the wake of teenage consumerism. Vandalism, hooliganism, mugging, baby-battering, homelessness all became familiar terms in the 1960s. At first these social problems were seen as discrete entities. The issue of homelessness, for example, brought graphically to life with the 'Cathy Come Home' TV drama documentary, was picked up and converted into a political issue by the formation of Shelter. In the year ending March 1966, Shelter had mobilised statistics to show nearly 3,000 children coming into care through homelessness and eviction. Parton (1985) catalogues a similar story with the creation and amplification of the social problem we know today as child abuse.

The publication of Abel-Smith and Townsend's *The Poor and the Poorest* in 1965 and of the DHSS document *Circumstances of Families* in 1967, converted a set of discrete problems into a demand for more comprehensive structural and potential change. Over a million families were living below the poverty line, as distinguished by supplementary benefit levels, and half a million children lived in families below the poverty line with the father in full-time work. The overwhelming problem was clearly not pathological, nor even contextual. It was structural. It was poverty.

The mobilisation of the social work lobby in support of political structural change was inevitable. It was also disastrous. In line with the move away from casework, many authorities had created community worker posts. It was in community work, with its connotations of hippies and long-haired socialists, that the politicisation of social work was identified. Social workers cannot bite the hand that feeds them and survive. Community Development Projects were set up to investigate the causes of poverty in the cities as a result of the 1967 DHSS report. By the time they reported, the political climate had changed. When the projects advocated structural changes in the distribution of wealth they were closed down. The loss of morale on social work was devastating.

Nonetheless community work continued to attract attention as a fringe activity. There is some evidence that the maintenance of community workers actually creamed off radical social work into an acceptable controlled situation, not unlike current co-option of militant users. In fact, community work in the 1960s was little more than family casework with the community as the client. It had not at that time developed either a rationale or a methodology.

Mainstream social work retained a more discrete profile, incorporating environmental awareness into what was still largely a counselling service. In practice this meant, for example, that if children came into care, they should be 'professionally assessed', with contributions on the home environment, school performance, psychological testing as well as residential reports. The emphasis shifted away from the centrality of the child to the child in the family context, with the development of family casework and the use of group work. It meant an emphasis too on preventing the reception of children into care due to avoidable environmental circumstances. The arrival of Section I money with the 1963 Children and Young Persons Act legitimated an increasing practice to pay out small sums of money to prevent children coming into care through financial difficulties. And increasingly child care officers found themselves in the role of service broker, negotiating with other agencies for discretionary or even statutory provision for their clients.

The battle for social work professionalism and with it, a more caring and liberal approach to treatment, was both won and lost with the 1969 Children and Young Persons Act. Technically the Act created care orders and intermediate treatment, and as such, gave the shape to most statutory work prior to the 1989 Children Act. Perhaps even more important was what it represented, namely the first orchestrated attempt by the profession to lobby for legislation. The result was that though the Act was passed, its implementation was not achieved. There was a backlash against it and in favour of more coercive measures.

While, for many, social work was seen as a 'soft option' to punishment, others inside the service realised that treatment was often more punitive than intended. Research indicated that social workers made more use of secure accommodation than courts had done before care orders came into being (Lemert 1967). Illich's (1973) 'radical non-intervention' suggested that kids did better if they were left to grow out of delinquent behaviour. The women's movement was becoming increasingly critical of established welfare (Wilson 1977). And then there was so much red tape.

In fact while social work was gearing itself up for the most co-ordinated and largest single front for welfare, the public was becoming more and more disillusioned with its results. Rather than solving social problems, social work seemed to be creating them, with 99,600 children in care in 1975 compared with 61,600 in 1956, and the problems of the inner cities coming to the fore with the Bristol riots in 1974. But it was reaction to the report on Maria Colwell that changed public opinion beyond all doubt. Maria died in 1973 at the age of seven, having been returned from foster parents to her own home by social workers.

Social work as a profession was not secure enough to take on this level of scandal. It was having its own private crisis of identity. With the apparent failure of casework and now community work, it came up with systems theory (the unitary method). Useful as a technique, it could not hold back the storm of protest.

Shooting the messenger became a familiar theme over the 1980s as one child care scandal broke after another. The irony was that in succeeding in establishing themselves as professionals, social workers had taken on responsibility for their clients far and beyond that on which they could deliver as agents of the state. By becoming advocates for their users, social workers had placed themselves alongside a group of outcasts, and found themselves in turn rejected. 'Dirty work' carries contamination with it; so much so that social workers were infected with the low status of their user group.

CONCLUSION

It seems likely that services created primarily in the interests of children would be shaped rather differently from the ones we have. For one thing, presumably they would treat the whole child, not his or her health, income, welfare, housing and education separately.

So whose interests do they serve? This brief historical overview suggests that services represent a compromise between five rather unequal interest groups: the professional, the state or elected state representatives, the community, the family and finally, the child. They represent a compromise too between different value systems of different interest groups at different points in time. Those value systems are not any value systems. Characteristically they are first ideal, second at best traditional, at worst, in a time warp. Services for children are, therefore, not only functional for those children but serve the wider community and society in which they operate. They are at one and the same time protective of vulnerable children and a deterrent to families deemed irresponsible.

This kind of service has consequences for children which are not always positive. Some of those consequences are:

- that some types of behaviour, and crucially not others, are labelled problematic;
- that children's services may fall victim to fads and fashions;
- that children's services can say more about moral panics and social problem construction than about the needs of children;
- that the construction of services by agencies into problem areas legitimates the public and professional agenda and thereby can exclude another agenda set by children and encompassing what they see as problematic;
- that children may be handled in groups according to their identified primary problem;
- that children may act as scapegoats for wider social problems.

The conclusion is that many of the 'failures' of child care services – the Jasmine Beckfords, the Gemma Hartwells, the Tyra Henrys – are not just accidents, though they are often that too. Rather they are representative of a fundamental conflict underpinning service provision.

The major aim of the legislation since 1933 has been the welfare and protection of children. In opposition to this, and what makes child care confusing, is the other major aim to control recalcitrant parents and deviant children. These two aims are represented along a continuum of service provision, which at one end makes a commitment to provide care in the community and at the other, to remove threats from that community. The result is that child care services are the site of institutionalised conflict between what have become known as the twin objectives of 'care' and 'control'. There is some room for manoeuvre along this continuum. There is, however, no breaking it since it represents the scope of the solution space available. Similarly, there are no answers to our three dilemmas; only some identification of the solution space and an evaluation of attempts to move within it with balance and with care.

The value of heritage is to understand history, and from that, to move forward. What implications does the heritage of care services have for managing these services? The answer is that how services are provided ultimately depends on what kind of service is wanted, why it is wanted, and for whom.

In the Victorian period it is very much the child who is rescued or punished. Gradually, with a greater understanding of the relationship between hereditary and environment, attention moves to the child in the family, reaching a peak in the late 1960s with the notion of the 'problem family'. In the early 1970s the whole community becomes the client, and then in the 1980s and early 1990s we get a swing back to the centrality of the child as represented first in the Beckford Report (1985) and finally in the Children Act (1989).

Managing for the user on behalf of others argues for a form of management and a kind of manager who does not need to be trained as a professional but who empathises with the rich tapestry that makes up the world that care services encompass and which includes professional practice. To empathise is difficult; much simpler to separate out professional from managerial practice. And yet what has been remarkable about care agencies is the capacity to juggle with the professional and the managerial, sometimes against all odds.

Balancing the inherent contradiction between parent, state, user and professional is increasingly being passed to managers. There is every reason to suppose this is a poisoned chalice. There is room for a new professionalism to emerge which treads more carefully the balance between responsibility and authority for and with users, a vacuum which is currently being filled by politicians, with uncertain success.

To achieve that, professionals will need to find ways of negotiating with other players in the system instead of telling them. For success in the market requires negotiation rather than an authority assumed out of expertise (Figure 7.1). To date professionals have tended to avoid negotiation. Rather they have put themselves above it, taking the moral high ground and arguing ethics and values. The result of that, sadly, has been to marginalise then in the new arena, and to hold back their own learning about their potential roles in that arena. It is not that values and ethics are not important. On the contrary, it is because thay are so important that they are non-negotiable. What that means is that professionals have to find other mechanisms and other products with which to trade. For trading operates at a middle level, and eventually the discussion about core values has to be translated into that middle level – into action – to be effective.

The role of the manager is not to replicate that of the professional. Neither is it to agree with the role of the professional. The role of the manager is to acknowledge the complex and competing values of the professional, the state, the elected representative and funder, the community, and user and to seek to represent them adequately in the management of the agency. Social work professionals, as others, do not have a premium on values or on caring. Their heritage to the manager is their persistent and valuable reminder of both those things.

REFERENCES

Abel-Smith, B. and Townsend, P. (1965), *The Poor and the Poorest*, London: Bell

Bowlby, J. (1970), *Child Care and the Growth of Love*, London: Penguin

Department of Health and Social Security (1967), *Circumstances of Families*, London: HMSO

Friedson, E. (1975), *The Profession of Medicine,* New York: Dead, Mead and Co.

Illich, I. (1973), 'The Professions as a kind of imperialism' in *New Society*, 13th Sept, pp. 633–5

Lemert, (1967), *Human Deviance, Social Problems and Social Control*

Parton, N. (1985), *The Politics of Child Abuse*, London: Macmillan

Wilson, L. (1977), *Women and the Welfare State*, London: Tavistock

CHAPTER FOUR

The heritage of work organisation

SUMMARY

Chapter 2 argued that public services are part of a delayed response, or set of responses to perceived demands of the environment. Chapter 3 added that those responses were interpreted through frameworks which were essentially competing, based on conflicting sets of assumptions and values, and related to time and place, and not necessarily with the outcome for the user most in mind. This chapter argues that the way in which caring services were organised was itself part of another heritage. The theory of organisations has a history too, as much a history of fashion and fad as any other.

The argument here is that public service organisations are by and large products of a model of organisation which dominated Britain during and after the Second World War and which is variously known as scientific management, the classical approach or Taylorism. It argues that the wholesale adoption of this particular model of organisations was influential in creating and maintaining the form of services we have come to know as the welfare state. It goes on to suggest that the model carried within itself the seeds of its own destruction in its dependence upon a production industry prototype arising out of an ideology grounded in Western capitalism. Combined with over-heavy bureaucratic processes built on at best to ameliorate industrial design faults, at worst through ill-conceived incrementalism, this model was inappropriate for service organisations and particularly so for public services. Organisational responses of the 1960s, 1970s and 1980s become in this interpretation a catalogue of attempts to deal with an organisational form in distress (chapter 5).

How was it that we ended up with the kind of public sector organisations we did within the welfare state? How did they influence the nature of the services delivered, and what made them particularly appropriate or inappropriate for this function? Above all, why have they been required to change so dramatically in the late 1980s and 1990s?

Organisations are products of their time and place. Public service organisations in the early 1990s may be described (variously) as organisations in transit or in trauma. Either way the changes being required of those organisations at this time are arguably different than any that have gone before. They are bigger in scale, faster in pace and cumulative or complex in nature and effect.

The writings of John Stewart (1986) have catalogued the ways in which such changes have come as a shock to organisations designed for stability, security and permanence. Stewart's Weberian approach has concentrated on the bureaucratic features of local authorities though much is transferable to other large public service organisations.

This chapter considers the influence of three major sets of organisational theory on the creation and maintenance of public service organisations. These are classical theory, the human relations approach and systems theory. It argues that though each has left an imprint upon the organisation of work in public service agencies, the primary influence has been that of the classical approach. The chapter goes on to link organisational theory with the ideologies of work which underpin it, and draws some conclusions about why organisations were required to change so dramatically in order to deliver user-oriented services.

A FRAMEWORK FOR UNDERSTANDING ORGANISATIONS

Figure 4.1 represents a framework for understanding organisations. It utilises the nomenclature of 1980s thinking which, in the absence of rigorous management theory, entered into received wisdom and became not only a description but a predictor of organisational behaviour. In it there is a clear (and ideal) connection between the organisation and the environment. The organisation is in the business of survival only if it pays attention to the requirements of the environment. To that end the model argues the organisation needs a view (or vision, or mission), overt or otherwise, about what it is in business to do, and a set of intentions (goals, strategies, plans, policies, objectives) designed to achieve that. The way in which that strategy works is to utilise the resources of the organisation (in public service agencies normally finance, staff, plant and time) through a

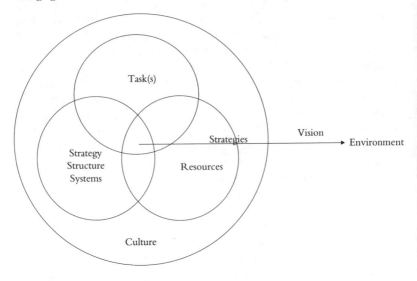

Figure 4.1   A framework for understanding organisations

set of processes (structures and systems) designed to achieve a number of preset tasks, some given by statute, some the result of rationing choices.

Like all models, it is flawed because it is at once simplified and based on improven assumptions. The laying out of alternative models, like that of Gareth Morgan (1986), arguably only removes the problem of analysis and selection one stage further.

To avoid undue theoretical discourse, therefore, Figure 4.1 is presented as the model to be used here as a framework for beginning to understand organisations of the 1980s. Created out of a combination of personal experience and theoretical study, it is presented simply as one conceptual tool which has proved 'good enough' for managers seeking to work on improving the functioning of organisations.

So much for the rational model of how organisations work. In practice of course, life isn't like that, and Figure 4.1 is useful only because it is a simple model, offering a basic language with which we can begin to understand the psychological, sociological and political heritage known as organisations theory and thereby construct more sophisticated and more realistic models of how organisations work in practice.

BUREAUCRACIES AND TAYLORISM

It is possible to trace the elements of bureaucracy back to the medieval church or even, if we are students of biblical history, to the Phoenicians. So it is not unexpected that it was in the organisation of religious practice that Weber (1963) found what he claimed to be the essentials of bureaucracy. These were power through authority rather than coercion (authority of person, of tradition and of role); hierarchy (the control of task through line relationships); and the division of labour (the fragmentation of work into separate jobs).

The bureaucratic model was personified in the UK in the Victorian legacy of the residential institution and hospital and later in William Morris's municipal socialism and the town hall. Not surprising then that the new welfare services emerging from those Victorian hospitals and from those town halls carried the stamp of bureaucracy.

But they carried more than that. For with the Second World War came the arrival of the assembly line, first in the numerous factories and then across the industrial scene. Arguably the working–class equivalent of bureaucracy, the assembly line faithfully reproduced Weber's three characteristics

The idea of the assembly line had become popularised through Henry Ford in America. Fascinated by the work of Taylor (1911), Ford had employed Taylor's methods to regulate efficient production of the motor car. The same methods were now used to control the introduction and management of largely unskilled and female labour into the munitions factories in the UK.

The idea was simple. A parallel was drawn between the workings of a steam engine and a production system. As the engine bearings run faster, so the governor rotates more quickly and closes off the supply of steam, creating a self-controlling system. Because the process was paralleled in an electrical circuit, it is often referred to as the 'black box model' (Figure 4.2).

Factories, it was assumed, could be created on the black box model such that measured imputs (labour, plant, raw materials, finance) could be processed in predetermined ways to produce fixed outputs or products. The level of quality of production could be regulated by means of a feedback loop which passed through a control system or series of control systems (such as supervisor, quality control system, budget holder) and which was able then to regulate future resource requirements.

Every idea has its moment. Though Taylor's definitive work was published in 1911, it found prominence in Britain during and after the Second World War. Supported by indigenous developments by Fayol in France (1916, translated 1949) and Mooney and Reilly in the United States the style became known collectively as the classical approach, finding support in a whole series of industrial sociologists such as Breth

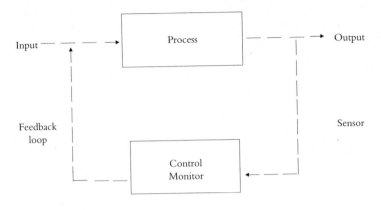

Figure 4.2 The black box model

(1957) and Allen (1958) and later and overwhelmingly in the business schools' derivation, Drucker's (1954) 'management by objectives'.

The classical approach had five major characteristics. The first was that work was determined by means of objectives from which task specification and targets would flow.

Second, labour was divided into specialist tasks in order to encourage particular skill development, save on time and training, maximise on scarce skills and so on. Tasks were analysed and ranked according to the degree of difficulty of performance and extent of discretion required. Workload measurement and quality monitoring ensured targets were met and hence objectives achieved.

Third, activities were grouped into functional units such as departments, the size and levels of which depended on various factors including economics of scale, capacity for effective coordination, the nature of the task and what came to be called the span of control. It was assumed that certain tasks, such as planning, were higher level activities and needed to be separated out from straight task supervision.

The fourth characteristic was that formal relationships were established between individuals as parts of functional units. Line relationships were established to create an identified chain of command for the purposes of accountability, communication and coordination. In addition, functional relationships across units facilitated achievement of a joint task. Lateral relationships were informal, distinguishing this system from a matrix structure. Personal assistants were established, with no other duty other than to assist the post holder or to deputise.

Finally, authority and responsibility were to go hand in hand. A guiding principle of the classical approach is that authority should be delegated as close to the task as possible and that authority should go with it on the basis that it is unreasonable to make someone responsible for something over which they have no authority. This neat 'accounting' attitude is typical of the approach overall, leading to tight job specifications and descriptions. In line with this, relationships between operational units were clearly specified, with operational staff in one section having no authority over those in another other than through a joint chain of command at the top of the hierarchy.

All in all, the intention and effect was to create task-driven organisations with the emphasis on the process of production, or the efficient conversion of imputs into outputs with minimum disruption or change.

It is difficult to over-estimate the influence of Taylorism on the construction of a post-war industrial Britain. It is even harder to imagine what the newly emerging National Health Service and Local Authority Children's Departments and later Seebohm's Social Services Departments would have looked like without this heritage. The departmental approach, the line management hierarchy, the separation of planning from supervision, the task specification according to function or user group, the specification of objectives from the top, and the delegation of authority are clearly the characteristics of health authorities and local authorities and of the large voluntary agencies who sought to imitate them. Indeed Taylorism and the classical school provided the ultimate rational process by which the monolithic and bureaucratic organisation personified in William Morris's municipal town hall could deliver services.

And that was just the problem. For Taylorism was essentially a production system, not a service system. A production system exists to deliver a product or set of agreed products to a customer. The level of specification of the product by the producer and by the customer varies according to the price of the article, the speciality of the products and the variation possible in the technology of production. At one level the technical customer may be able to specify a particular piece of technical equipment. At another ordinary customers simply take what is available or, in the jargon of the market place, get what they pay for.

In contrast, in a service system the customer is personally integrated into the production process, as Richard Normann (1984) points out. The customer in a restaurant does this by entering the restaurant, sitting at a table, consuming the goods and services of the establishment on the premises, and so on. Certainly it is usually the case that the choice available to the customer is determined by the menu or the character of the restaurant, and so there are similarities to the production process, the distinct difference being that the customer, in being part of the service delivery process, both influences the quality of that process, and makes it respond flexibly to change in demand and is, therefore, more likely to own the outcome. And indeed restaurant owners know this. They create an environment deliberately, which they call an ambience, as well as a choice of menu, aware that the response of the customers, and whether or not they enjoy the meal, is often as much to do with environment as eating good food.

The utilisation of a production model of work organisation for public sector services usefully allowed rationed and rational systems of care to emerge with the welfare state. It also had some major and unintended consequences.

Users of service became raw material, described by their conditions and sifted and categorised arguably according to the routine procedures of the agency rather than their own needs. Once integrated into the system, users were processed at the discretion of the agency. Files were opened and case numbers allocated for each user. Users at once became unequal; something was done to them rather than with them. Once categorised (often into a 'first-fit' category) users were identified by their category (e.g. disability), a process which in turn generates the need for subsequent 'normalisation' strategies. Not surprisingly maximum rewards (home visits, benefits in kind) came from colluding with the categorisation and the processes designed to deal with it, known ironically in the trade as client 'manipulation'.

First-line management in this system became a task of maintenance control avoiding disruption or 'noise' on the system. Behaviour which did disrupt the system became crises for the agency (not necessarily for the user). The system was easier to control if extraneous noise was minimised, so the system was not conducive to influence from outside. Interagency work for instance, or work with elected members can be seen as potentially disruptive. Successful processing may even be at the expense of the user's own helping network, resulting in further applications for assistance.

The system found it easier to batch its processing arrangements. So old people, people with learning difficulties, children at risk, people with the same illness were put together, sometimes literally in the form of residential provision, not necessarily through their own choice, but arguably for the convenience of the system.

Finally, the separation of monitoring and control from the process of service delivery had the effect of splitting the manager from the practitioner and assuming that the one had control over the other. Each could blame the other, both unable to see noise outside the system as anything other than interference. These are not problems of professional practice or of management but simply of an organisational design in which bureaucratic efficiency has been confused with best practice (James 1984).

Arguably the methods employed in the late 1980s and early 1990s to create a contracting culture have involved a return to the five major characteristics of the classical approach (objective setting, skill mixing, restructuring according to task, chain of command and clear accountability). The black box model bears striking resemblance to the Audit Commission's (1985) model of performance evaluation (input, process, output and outcome) (James 1987). And the separation of task from its control, and supervision remains at the root of the debate between professional discretion and managerial accountability.

With hindsight on the 1980s, it was as if breaking up the estate required us first to put our house in order. That is not to criticise adversely activities which represented serious if unsatisfactory attempts to control major turbulence on the system. In retrospect the activities were less important in themselves than for the change in culture which they bridged towards more user-sensitive services. And the dominance of the Classical Model continues to explain some of the resistance and inertia to change that remains within our large public service organisations.

THE HUMAN RELATIONS SCHOOL

Taylorism may have been the dominant model in organisational design and hence in developing a view of what management is and what managers do. But it was not the only model. There was another view that looked for its heritage to Durkheim, to Marx, and to other aspects of Weberian theory. It was personified in Elton Mayo (MacGregor 1960) and what came to be known as the Human Relations School. Durkheim (1858-1917), looking at the relationship between work and social structure in the wake of the Industrial Revolution was struck by what he called 'Anomie': the normlessness and social isolation of individuals operating in a world in which traditional culture and community had broken down in favour of urbanisation (Durkheim 1952). Marx too had a theory that said that human life needs vitality and involvement and reproduction in order to grow. For him the labour process generated by capitalism separated workers from the product of their own work and this in turn caused alienation in workers from their work, from their fellow workers, and ultimately from themselves. Weber, as father of the Action or *Verstehende* school in sociology, stressed the significance of free will and the individual's ultimate control over his or her own destiny. For Weber, quality of life, and particularly life at work, might be determined to some extent by life chances, but his study of the ideal types of leadership and his 'Great Men of History' thesis led him to believe that vocation, charisma and leadership could always transcend environmental constraint.

For Elton Mayo it was not accomplishment of a task that achieved the business of the organisation, as with Frederick Taylor, but the way the staff performed that task. Best known for his work at the Western Electric Company's Hawthorne plant near Chicago, Mayo experimented with the effect of light on production levels. To his surprise he found that production levels rose whatever the level of light. In other words it was taking interest in the work that counted. More than this, future experiments demonstrated that production rose as a result of being part of a work group under scrutiny: the famous Hawthorne effect. Moving on then to interview techniques, he found that even the opportunity for people to talk about their jobs raised work levels. These interviews revealed that working conditions did matter to staff and that human relations between workers and with supervisors were apparently at least as important to staff as wages.

Out of this Mayo went on to study group process. He saw the slacking identified by Taylor, but found the explanation for it not in laziness but in very complex networks of informal goals and informal rules that permeated and separated different groups of workers in the organisation and which resulted in group norms of performance. He identified the notion of 'morale' to describe motivation levels, finding that new members to a group rapidly adopted measures of adjustment in output to achieve an equilibrium. For him, management was not about control, as it was for Taylor. He found control was already very much in place. The trick for him was to harness levels of motivation to create expectations of higher levels of output. Managers, therefore, must not just train workers in technical skills, but must address in addition the attitudes and behaviours both of the individual and of the work team. This was a whole new conception of management. It was embryonic of the view that management is about the how as much as the what: about people as much as task.

Mayo's views were developed by the work of Maslow (1954), amongst others, into the self-actualisation or human relations school. For them work was a means by which self actualisation was achieved, a view far apart from Taylor's instrumentalism where work was a means to achieving a wage packet. The responsibility of the manager is to provide a clear policy context within which individual groups can find their own way with certain checks and balances in the form of individual appraisal and staff development. Authority becomes authority over people, not over tasks, with influence a more effective route to change than discipline.

Because the group is the unit of production there is an emphasis on participative decision making within it and of liaison with groups outside it. The notion of linchpins, gatekeepers or boundary people emerges with Likert (1961) and the identification of superordinate goals which bind groups together, a concept that emerged later as the climate or culture of the organisation.

Structurally there is an acceptance of informal goals and networks alongside formal ones. The hierarchy is to be as flat as possible to assist communication across the organisation with extensive decentralisation intended to foster low-level entrepreneurship and prevent over-differentiation between sections and units. In contrast, job enlargement, job swaps and job rotation are intended to promote shared learning and matrix responsibility. Leadership stops being described as a set of personality traits or a position accorded by privilege of ownership, wealth or connection, and starts becoming something about generating motivation and enthusiasm which in turn is the rationale behind 'management by walking about'. Work groups are powerhouses of synergistic energy waiting to be released. Team-building becomes essential. As Taylor became the proforma for 'management by objectives', so Mayo modelled Peters and Waterman's (1982) excellent companies.

Talk of self-actualisation, of vocation, of doing your own thing, fitted well with an era of the Beatles and a teenage population educated to believe they could achieve outside class boundaries, or at any rate, beyond their parents' wildest dreams. It continued to fit well as those 1960s teenagers became chief executives of public service companies in their 40s. But the human relations school never competed significantly with the classical approach. Experience suggested it needed a boom economy to finance it (an experience denied by Peters and Waterman to their acute embarrassment as their 'excellent' companies folded). Even the Volvo factory at Kalmar, heralded as a showpiece when it was built to produce cars with teams working collectively in bays, could, if times were hard, be physically reshaped to revert to the assembly line, though this fact remained a closely guarded secret.

Nonetheless the emphasis on human relationships, on work groups, on leadership and on delegated decision making fitted easily with health and social care service perspectives. Where East Sussex and Normanton Social Services thought they had invented decentralisation in the 1970s, they were in fact reproducing what was already emerging by then in industry as a way of organising service delivery. And in fact industry had already moved on to embrace systems theory.

SYSTEMS THEORY

Organisational theory is a hybrid product. The earliest management consultants were the industrial sociologists often brought in by American companies eager to improve performance and often conducting their own research on the back of company contracts. (Some might say times haven't changed!) Taylor and his companies were among this breed. In contrast, Mayo and his colleagues grew out of an emergent interest in the psychology of work, developing social psychology or the study of behaviour in groups.

A third approach grew out of biology and the physical sciences and engineering. This was systems theory. Systems theory itself had many strands. On the one hand Stafford Beer (1975) was promoting management cybernetics, applying systems approaches to control and communication problems and arriving at notions which have now matured as systems analysis in management information systems. On the other hand Ackoff (1974) was developing operational research, the precursor to work study and ergonomics. Meanwhile Bertalanffy (Bertalanffy and Laviolette 1981), the biologist, was into general systems theory or the application of systems theory to growth and evolution, into ecosystems and organic models of organisations.

All strands talked about flows, about communication, about boundaries, about synergy and above all, what was seen as an holistic approach to solving organisational problems. It makes more sense, therefore, to talk of a systems approach than a systems theory. Organisations were body corporates, sets of interconnected parts of an organic whole where pressure on any one part might be felt elsewhere. In this organic view response to change is at two levels. On the one hand the organisation resists radical change, tending to modify it towards its stable state (homoeostasis) in order to survive in its existing form (or species). On the other hand the organisation adapts to incremental change relatively easily by a process of evolution, encouraging differentiation across the organisation to suit environmental pressures. This latter response was developed by Galbraith (1980) and Argyris and Schön (1978) in the notion of organisational learning. A healthy organisation is one that learns from its own behaviour and adapts accordingly.

The organic model of organisations sees the organisation as a human body. Though symbolically clear, the model suffers from over-literal translation. There is no logic behind the symbolism and no theoretical evidence for it. Indeed it can be argued that homoeostasis was a function of a stable environment which created stable organisations, rather than a characteristic of organisations themselves. As such the notion of homoeostasis may well have contributed to the misconception that radical change is an unnecessary feature of organisational life.

More robust models using systems theory are under development by Peter Checkland (1981) and Brian Wilson (1986) at the only Department of Systems in the UK at Lancaster University and by Peter Senge (1992) in the United States.

WORK ORGANISATION AND IDEOLOGY

Organisation theory, like all other theory, operates at different levels of analysis. At the everyday level, for instance, the organic approach to management works: it helps to regard the organisation as a corporate body which needs to work in harmony in order to achieve. At the theoretical level, however, the model does not hold up; it is nothing more than an image. The same goes for systems theory. It is useful to think of organisational problems as problems of communication between systems, whether those systems are overt, like departmental structures, or covert, like informal networks. It is useful because it helps the manager to get on with the problem. But again, systems theory does not go beyond this; it does not, for example, explain why or how system boundaries were formed in the first place. It does not tackle why effective communication is necessary.

In contrast, the scientific management or classical approach and the human relations approach are theories of a different order. They are of a different order because they arise out of conceptual frameworks or ideologies. Scientific management is part of a rational, deductive paradigm or *weltanschauung* (world view). It is a top-down view of the universe, where tasks and rules are management given and worker received. Often mistakenly called a consensus view of management, it assumes that those at the top know best and that their view will carry throughout the organisation. It assumes that organisations exist to perform a task or set of tasks, and it concentrates on the performance of those tasks to achieve maximum output.

In other words it is instrumental in approach. It is often called the control model because it identifies management with control and because problems are inevitable regarded as control problems. The workplace is a closed system and relations with the environment are as limited as possible in order to maximise control and avoid disruption. Work has to be organised in certain ways because of the technology involved. In the factory this may be the assembly line or equivalent; in the bureaucracy it

53

is the line management structure. Work organisation is, therefore, economically and technologically determined.

Ideologically the concept is located in the rationalism of Western capitalism according to Marx. Marx suggested that the greatest potential for profit existed in increasing technology or controlling wage levels such that more productivity is achieved per worker. He goes on to emphasise the effects of this process on worker's attitudes to irregular and uncertain work. Where people are valued only for their labour, certain conclusions can be drawn about non-productive members of the family such as the elderly, sick, disabled, children and carers.

This crude Marxism is modified by what Wedderburn and Craig (1975) see as paternalistic concern for working conditions. Lockwood (Goldthorpe *et al.* 1968) points out that the worker and the consumer are one and the same anyway, suggesting that the worker has as much influence on the product as the consumer. The point remains however that jobs are worker-received rather than worker-determined, a process reinforced by socialisation processes according to Lockwood. Indeed Goldthorpe *et al.* (1968) see wage spiralling as one attempt to compensate for low job satisfaction and Ashton (1975) sees the workplace as a major source of self-identity in terms of class and status.

One effect of the division of labour, in its search for uniformity and order, is to standardise work contributions and thereby fail to value entrepreneurship and innovation. Its reinforcement of job boundaries precludes holistic approaches to problem solving except at the higher levels.

The hierarchical system works in the same way: it reinforces that some workers are always at the top and others at the bottom. As such it legitimates and socialises people into inequality. Habermas (1976) recognises this when he says that work organisation is politically not technologically determined: it is directed to upholding the power of the dominant group, be they owner, managers and/or professionals. In this interpretation constant restructuring is simply one mechanism for making explicit the power struggles over profit or over survival between interest groups. The position of certain groups at the top of the hierarchy means that their views and their social values filter down and become accepted by the rest of the organisation as desirable and, therefore emerge as consensus views. Because the same kind of groups/people tend to be at the top of all large organisations (i.e. other professionals, other managers, other owners) these views become collectively hegemonic in character.

In its generous and consensus form, the filtering down process is paternalistic; the 'leaders' create dependence in the workers by the dispensing of approved benefits (such as promotion or wage increases) and thereby legitimate themselves as leaders. In its less generous and conflict form, the leaders use the workplace to instil order in what would otherwise be regarded as a rabble. Unless workers are organised and controlled they are seen as without purpose; lack of order is identified with lack of responsibility. This is the thinking that created both the nineteenth century workhouse and Thatcher's work experience programmes.

The main rival to the instrumental approach is the self-actualisation model of work organisation. Identified here particularly with Elton Mayo and the human relations school, this model finds its ideological root variously in the Puritan tradition of self-enhancement, the Greek and Eastern traditions of harmony of body and soul and the romantic utilitarianism, of C Wright Mills (1959). It sees work not as a necessary evil inflicted on Adam and Eve in punishment, but as a primary source of satisfaction. As such it emphasises the work itself rather than its output. The main problem with the model is its limited capacity for application within a western framework. As Maslow (1954) pointed out, self-actualisation is an ideal to be aimed for when all other needs are satisfied. And although Trist (1973) argues that job satisfaction increases productivity, the inclusion of areas of discretion conflicts overwhelmingly with the need to standardise work processes in organisations designed fundamentally on instrumental lines.

Traditional organisation theory sees the instrumental and self-actualisation models as polarised. In practice, however, there are a whole range of compromises between the two, including Marshall's (1981) welfare capitalism in the UK, Trist's sociotechnical approach and Schumacher's (1973) alternative technology strategy.

The most powerful compromise is the set of hypotheses known as 'contingency theory'. Not a theory at all but simply a pragmatic guide to action, contingency theory is a strategy mobilised first by Quinn (1980) as 'logical incrementalism' and by Lindblom (1959) as 'muddling through'. Grounded in an empirical inductive model rather than a theoretical deductive one, it argues that most decisions made in organisations are incremental, made according to circumstances and not with reference to grand theory. This is opportunism at its best, with an eye to creativity, and to be distinguished from the failure to make any decision at all.

CONCLUSIONS

To return to Figure 4.1 for a moment, it could be said that each of the major models and theories of organisational behaviour under review have sought to intervene in organisational life from a different perspective. The classical approach intervened on Task, in its present form in variations of Drucker's (1954) management by objectives. The human relations approach intervened on Resources, most especially human resources, and arguably its modern equivalents intervene on Culture. The systems approach intervened in the processes by which services were delivered, altering structure, information and communication systems, an approach which still holds major appeal to legislators and managers. Contingency theory argued that intervention is according to opportunity, be that on task, on structure and systems, on resources or on culture or any combination of those.

And more recently Peters and Waterman (1982) and their co-patriots intervened in Culture. For if you cannot clarify Task, cannot control Resources, cannot deliver Systems, you can, they thought, achieve them all through the control of Hearts and Minds: Vision, Mission, Values and Leadership.

The dominant heritage of classical theory has been in its rational approach to defining management. Organisations are, or should be in this view, orderly set-ups where the best people are at the top and where everybody knows their place. Managing is primarily about achieving task, and the good manager is the one who directs people clearly and objectively to achieve that task.

Alongside classical theory are threads of other traditions. These traditions see organisations as essentially units of power and potentially of privilege and therefore potentially chaotic, certainly unclear. Managing is essentially about helping people create processes for the effective completion of the task. It is about people and it is a political activity.

In conclusion, the classical tradition has made a significant and valuable contribution to the effective organisation of public services. Its methods and its ideology are, however, at variance with the management of empowerment. You cannot run a top-down control organisation and expect staff, and through them, users, to be empowered. To do so requires a different concept of management.

REFERENCES

Ackoff, R.L. (1974), *The Systems Revolution in Long Range Planning*, vol 7, no 6, pp. 2–5

Allen, L.A. (1958), *Management and Organization*, New York: McGraw-Hill

Argyris, C. and Schön, D.A. (1978), 'What is an organisation that it may learn?' in *Organisational Learning*, Mass.: Addison-Wesley

Ashton, D.N. (1975), 'The transition from school to work' in Esland, G. *et al.* (eds) *People and Work*, Holmes McDougal and OU Press

Audit Commission (1985), *Good Management in Local Government*, London: HMSO

Beer, S. (1975), *Designing Freedom*, New York: J. Wiley

Bertalanffy, L. von and Laviolette, P. (1981), *Systems View of Man*, United States: Westview

Checkland, P. (1981), *Systems Thinking, Systems Practice*, Chichester: J. Wiley

Drucker, P. (1954), *The Practice of Management*, New York: Harper and Bros

Durkeim, E. (1897, translated 1952) *Suicide*, London: Routledge and Kegan Paul

Fayol, H. (1916/1949), *General and Industrial Management*, London: Pitman

Galbraith, J.R., (1980), in Lockilt, M. and Spear, R. (eds), *Organisational Design: an information processing view in organisations as systems*, Stratford: OU Press

Goldthorpe, J.H., Lockwood, D., Bechhofer, F. and Platt, J. (1968), *The Affluent Worker: Industrial Attitudes and Behaviour*, Cambridge: Cambridge University Press

Habermas, J. (1976), *Legitimation Crisis*, London: Heinemann

James, A. (1984), 'Community care under Thatcher: work organisation and ideology' (unpublished paper)

James, A. (1987), 'Planning and performance', *Social Services Insight*, 6 March

Likert, R. (1961), *The Principle of Supportive Relationships in Organisational Theory* (ed) Pugh, D.S., London: Penguin and (1961) *New Patterns in Management*, New York: McGraw-Hill

Lindbolm, C.E. (1959), 'The science of muddling through', *Public Administration Review*, vol 1, Spring, reproduced in Pugh, D.S. (ed) (1971) *Organisation Theory: Selected readings*, London: Penguin

MacGregor, D. (1960), *The Human Side of Enterprise*, New York: McGraw-Hill

Marshall, T.H. (1981), *Right to Welfare and other essays*, Aldershot: Gower

Maslow, A.H. (1954), *Motivation and Personality*, New York: Harper

Morgan, G. (1986), *Images of Organisation*, London: Sage

Normann, R. (1984), *Service Management: Strategy and Leadership in Service Business*, Chichester: J. Wiley

Peters, T.J. and Waterman, R.H. (1982), *In Search of Excellence*, New York: Harper & Row

Quinn, J.B. (1980), *Strategies for Change, Logical Incrementalism*, Illinois: Irwin

Schumacher, E.F. (1973), *Small is Beautiful: Economics as if People Mattered*, New York: Harper and Row

Senge, P.M. (1992), *Fifth Discipline: Art and Practice of the Learning Organisation*, Business Books

Stewart, J. (1986), *The New Management of Local Government*, London: Allen and Unwin

Taylor, F.W. (1911), *The Principles of Scientific Management*, New York: Harper

Trist, E.L. (1973), 'A Socio-technical critique of scientific management' in Edge, D.O. and Wolfe, S.N. (1973), *Meaning and Control: essays in social aspects of science and technology*, pp. 95–116, London: Tavistock

Weber, M. (1963), *The Sociology of Religion*, London: Tavistock

Wedderburn, D. and Craig, C. (1975), 'Relative deprivation in work' in Esland, G. *et al.* (eds) *People and Work*, Holmes McDougal and OU Press

Wilson, B. (1986), *Systems: Concepts, Methodologies and Applications*, Chichester: J. Wiley

Wright Mills, C. (1959), *Sociological Imagination*, New York: Oxford University Press

CHAPTER FIVE

The Thatcher years

INTRODUCTION AND SUMMARY

How do you control runaway public expenditure and address enhanced demands for services within a strong ideological framework without alienating the voters? This was the dilemma which underpinned Thatcher's interventions across the pubic service sector in the late 1970s and through the 1980s.

This chapter argues that the changes demanded of the public service sector in the Thatcher era, though led by financial constraints at the rational, practical, everyday level were, in hindsight, driven primarily by political will. Clearly the political mandate depended, as always, on perceived economic 'success', so demonstration of this was very important. Indeed control of public expenditure was a necessary part of the government's strategy to regain control of the economy as a whole. However, the ways in which changes in the public sector were achieved, though demonstrating a range of imaginative techniques, were fundamentally about retaining political control at Westminster. Public services were to be the arena in which the centralist state demonstrated power and authority over the local state.

To take a couple of examples to demonstrate the point: the introduction of CCT (compulsory competitive tendering), worked for the government at a number of levels. At one level it induced competition into public service, arguing that the introduction of market mechanisms would increase efficiency. But at another level, separating out the provision and commissioning of services and requiring tender processes between them split the concentrated and monopolistic power of local authorities. It did so not by invitation, not by request, but by statute. As such it was arguably a demonstration of power by a centralist state. It said very clearly that not all services provided by local authorities deserve to be public or deserve to be monopolistic in character. As such it renegotiated the boundaries between what is public and what is private and redefined the business of local government without declared forms of consultation. It was, in other words, as much about political control as about economics.

LMS (local management of schools) is another such example. While arguably enhancing parental choice over school entry and parental control through the use of parent-governors, one of the major effects of LMS was to decimate the budget of local education committees and hence of county councils and metropolitan boroughs. In making direct deals with parents and with heads of schools through LMS, the government was by-passing traditional, if arguably unsatisfactory, forms of electoral representation. The delegation of staffing budgets to heads of schools put professionals-turned-managers (rather than local authorities) in charge of other professionals. Combined with a national curriculum, this served to constrain the activities and behaviours of ordinary teachers both inside and outside the classroom. Never again would left-wing local authorities have the potential to combine with teaching professionals to disrupt education as had happened with the teachers' strikes of the 1980s.

For power and, therefore, control to be redistributed in favour of central government three features needed to be in place. Not surprisingly those features were common to all the debates across the public service sector in the Thatcher era, and are, therefore, worthy of further consideration. They are:

- the redefinition of what was public and what was private responsibility;
- realignment of central–local relations;
- revised financial and political accountabilities.

THE PUBLIC–PRIVATE DEBATE

When Thatcher came to power there was a consensus that education, health, the public utilities, the criminal justice system, the civil service, and to a much less extent housing, were public services to be publicly provided. By the end of the 1980s, in just a decade, that was not the case.

It was by then possible, indeed desirable, to separate the aims of service outcomes from the means of delivery. Publicly owned aims (mass

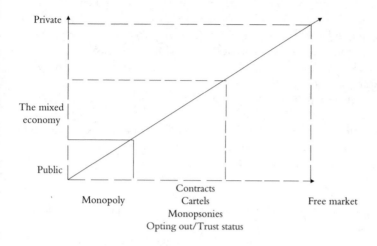

Figure 5.1 The Thatcher agenda

education, clean water, etc) could be achieved through a range of providers in the public, private and independent sectors.

How did this major shift in perception and behaviour came about? Two factors are critical: the experience of declining public sector provision and the transfer of service provision to the market place through a mixed economy of care.

Figure 5.1 illustrates the Thatcher agenda. Ideologically Thatcherism sat very uncomfortably upon a public sector platform constituted according to post-war collectivism. If there was a crisis in the welfare state, it was less one of welfare than of statism, that is of controlling the spending and increased bureaucracy of local services in line with resource constraints.

The post-war welfare state had allegedly been founded on rights: the right to work, the right to housing, the right to health and so on. In fact it had arguably been founded on privilege as much as on right (e.g. gender). The crisis in funding combined with disillusionment over accessing services now forced rationing decisions into the public arena. One of the outcomes was a crisis of confidence in the means of existing service delivery systems to manage the overload effectively. If there was a crisis of welfare, this was it. Another was confusion over values that had traditionally associated public services with public service providers or the public good with public means of delivery.

Thatcher's attempts to shift public service into a free market economy, where private provision would compete equally with the public and voluntary sectors, was initially strongly resisted by the public sector. It was clear, however, that the public sector was not going to be allowed – and not going to be sufficient – to continue its monopoly of service provision, a monopoly arguably led by professional and administrative interests. The rapid disintegration of public sector provision, real, imagined or constructed artificially through underfunding and overspending, quickly attuned all but the most intransigent Labour-held local authorities to a half-way house known as 'the mixed economy of care'. Variously called 'partnership' in the Probation Service, and 'healthy alliances' in the NHS, and the 'market-testing' in the Prison Service, the mixed economy of care brought together different parts of public sector services with each other and with voluntary and private sector providers.

How the problem was defined or socially constructed was crucial to acceptance of the mixed economy. If the problem, as defined by Thatcher, was that of the 'burden of welfare' on a restricted national economy, then the use of private or voluntary investment or provision could swell the range of services available for rich and poor alike. If, to continue the Thatcher argument, the issue was how to regenerate the economy, then bleeding, in the form of human service provision, only delayed or threatened that process.

For after all doesn't wealth creation have a trickle-down effect that in good time would ensure everyone could purchase services according to need? But if, as intransigent socialists claimed, the issue was not wealth creation but the degeneration of collective responsibility and an uncaring state, then would not investment or provision by private or voluntary agencies only speed that process up? Ideological resolution was impossible. The success of the notion of the mixed economy (that is, that services might be provided by public, private and voluntary organisations, creating a mixed market) was that it could encompass a range of opinions.

Moreover, at the practical level, it seemed to work. If elderly people were prepared to seek out and meet their own accommodation needs in the private sector in preference to local authority establishments, then that was their choice. The fact that that choice was unequally subsidised by the Department of Social Security came out only later with the Audit Commission's (1986) identification of 'perverse incentives'.

Where Thatcher was mistaken, and what contributed to her removal from the premiership was in her judgement of the electorate. The vast majority of people within the UK continued to want a welfare state, in that they wanted education, health, income support, and so on to be provided as a function of citizenship. This came out strongly during the

1992 Election campaign in relation to the NHS. The market place would not suffice as the basic determinant of social goods and services.

Basic rights could be supplemented by privileges of purchase. Many people were in fact not only prepared to pay directly as individuals for the purchase of some services (e.g. insurance and pensions), but actually preferred to do so. But privatisation of what were seen as basic welfare rights was unacceptable. The social market, expressed as a mixed economy of care, was as far as the electorate were ready to go. So, for example, John Major in his election campaign, had to reassure the electorate that trust status providers remained within the NHS and were not privatised.

Opening public sector services to private sector influence had payoffs. First of all the public services had to face up to their own inadequate stereotypes of private sector organisations as crudely driven by profit. In fact they found themselves accessing a whole range of different and fluid organisational types, from the small business to the franchise to the large firm. There was much to learn from the private sector also about listening to customers, about assuring for quality, about strategy and marketing, about investing in staff development and in user-friendly information systems.

The public sector also had much to share with the private sector, including a heritage of rights and responsibilities to users whose background was one of collective disadvantage and misrepresentation. They had a set of values, or principles, that implied working to outcomes over and above satisfaction of the individual consumer or the individual transaction, and a need to protect choices with and on behalf of groups of people who were not always vocal and were often minorities.

Finally both had much to learn about working together. If competition was to be healthy, and not a substitute for territorialism, then there had to be much more clarity about the function of services and their accountability to users, to politicians and to service funders. There had to be some acceptance that joint working, even within the public sector, had not been successful in general to date and that a variety of relationships were needed to achieve within a mixed economy.

REALIGNMENT OF CENTRAL–LOCAL RELATIONS

One of the paradoxes of the changes taking place in the Thatcher era was the dual presence of centralisation and decentralisation. The state was centralising by reassuming control at Westminister. It achieved this through the use of legislation, through revised funding mechanisms, through the displacement or trading off of professional power, and through the making of direct deals with the user or with private or voluntary sector providers which bypassed the local statutory organisation.

Before Thatcher, public service legislation followed an established if tardy pattern of working parties, working documents, Green Papers, White Papers and finally bills. Where consent was forthcoming, for example over the Children Act, this process was still followed. Indeed the NHS and Community Care Act of 1990 was arguably a model of effective consultation, its delays due to Thatcher's distaste for naming local authorities as lead authorities rather than to lack of consent among key agencies. Where consent was not forthcoming, or was to be achieved at high speed, the process provided endless opportunities to confound and frustrate legislation as Thatcher had learned very early on with Norman Fowler's attempt at a Social Security Bill. The result was that legislation generally began to assume a more aggressive stance.

The Probation Service Green Paper, *Supervision and Punishment in the Community: A Framework for Action* (1990), for example followed an Audit Commission review and required the service to move 'centre-stage' in dealing with offenders. It combined this invitation with a warning that alternatively a new agency could be established to take responsibility for more serious offenders. At the same time the traditional 80:20 ratio of funding between the Home Office and local authorities was called into question. The clear implication was that unless local Probation Services toed the line, they would be 100 per cent dependent upon the Home Office and arguably lose their local base. Challenges to professional authority included National Standards and a review of qualifying training. And finally, deals were struck which bypassed the service, notably with NACRO (National Association for Care and Resettlement of Offenders), symbolised in June 1990 by a place in the Honour's list for its director.

The result was that an outmoded and recalcitrant Probation Service was quickly knocked into shape. The Decision Document that followed, *Organising Supervision and Punishment in the Community* (1991), was much more conciliatory, similarly followed by the Decision Document *Partnership in Dealing with Offenders in the Community* (1992) which neatly institutionalised the notion of the mixed economy within the Probation Service within a period of two years.

Though the process was aggressive in the extreme, it worked with the Probation Service to an extent not paralleled in other public services. First the services had an expanding budget which was not at that stage cash limited and therefore was without the malaise arising from cuts in service. Low turnover within the service led to a Chief Officer population which knew and worked with each other well and included an ACOP (Association of Chief Officers of Probation) group eager to learn and improve management of the service. And finally a history of direct relationships with the Home Office, now enhanced by a stable civil service staff and a long serving minister, paid off.

It was not however, the Probation Service which was the problem to central government. It was rather a rising, and increasingly costly, prison population which threatened the law and order lobby and which was not being addressed by the magistracy or the judiciary. How much easier to chip away at the Probation Service, perhaps with some revision to the professional practice of solicitors and barristers, than take on the judiciary.

If at one level the state was centralising, at another it was decentralising. A cynical view could be that the centre was giving away problems (usually financial) that it could not handle (viz the 'poisoned chalice' of community care being passed to local authorities). A more generous view would be that, with planning and evaluation mechanisms in place, the centre could afford local variation and local choice. For the fact remained that though some may disagree ideologically with Thatcherism, and others find the process of change in the public sector speeded up to an unacceptable pace, few could dispute the value of the techniques brought in to manage a revised set of services.

It was as if there were a pack of cards dealt out to every service: each pack was identical but their order of stacking and the use to which they were put by the players varied between services (Figure 5.2). The process usually began from the Treasury, with services addressed, with hindsight quite appropriately, according to size of budget and ease of pickings. Housing came first therefore, followed by education, the public utilities, the Health Service, the Probation Service and finally and potentially Social Security and the criminal justice system.

Enquiries about Value for Money or the 3Es (Economy, Efficiency, Effectiveness) from the Treasury to the appropriate spending department were passed on to the service, usually initiating a review process by a quango such as the Audit Commission. Effective review required the establishment of indicators, policy and procedural guides and business plans against which performances could be measured. These in turn required clear accountabilities for staff in meeting agreed targets, resulting in job evaluation, revised job descriptions and inspection and quality assurance systems. With tasks and accountabilities clarified, some could be contracted out to other providers in the system or the private and voluntary sector.

Sanctions (such as Compulsory Competitive Tendering, C.C.T.) and incentives (such as government-subsidised specific grants for authorities

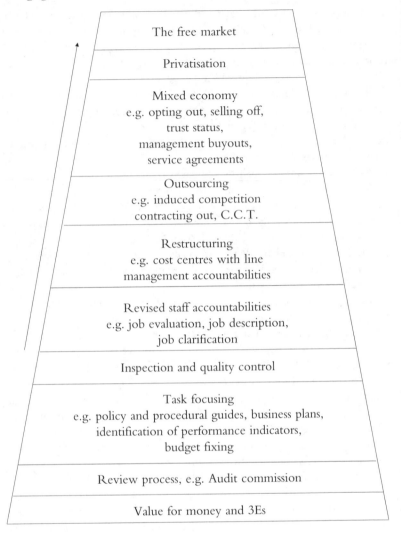

The free market

Privatisation

Mixed economy
e.g. opting out, selling off,
trust status,
management buyouts,
service agreements

Outsourcing
e.g. induced competition
contracting out, C.C.T.

Restructuring
e.g. cost centres with line
management accountabilities

Revised staff accountabilities
e.g. job evaluation, job description,
job clarification

Inspection and quality control

Task focusing
e.g. policy and procedural guides, business plans,
identification of performance indicators,
budget fixing

Review process, e.g. Audit commission

Value for money and 3Es

Figure 5.2 The stack of cards

which could afford to take them up) reinforced this process. Reorganisation took the form of redundancies and restructuring into decentralised cost centres with budget delegation extended as far as pump-priming non-statutory provision, as with the home help and home care services. A variety of opt-out arrangements were experimented with, including management buyout, opting out, selling off, transfer into offshore companies (usually of charitable status), contracting out and application for trust status. Most of these techniques fell short of privatisation, other than for the public utilities which were sold off to the public in shares.

In Social Services departments, for example, a funding system which was essentially political in character and relied on bids and counterbids, was overlaid with rationing processes designed to achieve value for money. Increasing availability of information technology held out a false promise of rational decision-making based on indicators of performance. These indicators included statutory requirements, policy and procedural statements, mission statements and sets of objectives such that by the mid-1980s at least one enterprising department was selling client group policy guides.

Identification of core businesses in Social Services led to restructuring around those businesses, namely back from patch to client groups and then back to adult/children services. It was accompanied by mechanisms designed to make staff accountable for core tasks, through job descriptions, appraisal and budget holding. Decentralised units were encouraged to identify with local community initiatives, often interprofessional, sometimes voluntary or private in character. With pressure from politicians to slough off units requiring capital investment, it was not long before some became independent or took on charitable status. This was privatisation by the back door.

There was inevitably some sharp practice. There is a fine line between entrepreneurship and deviance. The continuous process of removing doublechecks and balances in order to free up management in a political context had its causalities. In one notorious authority the child protection team left *en bloc* and was pump-primed to set up in private practice. It then hired itself back to the authority at doubled rates. In general, however, the employment of the management techniques led to more clarity about rationing services.

If the understanding and employment of new management techniques was difficult, it was not as problematic as dealing with the profound sense of powerlessness experienced by many staff trying to grapple with what felt like a barrage of criticism against public services which regarded themselves as underfunded and fundamentally worthy. As with many organisations under stress the values of care agencies imploded such that they became, like their clients, vulnerable in what they perceived to be a hostile world.

For those at the centre, decentralisation was experienced as loss of power and control. The introduction of business plans, community care plans and client group strategies (e.g. All-Wales Strategy on Mental Health) could be conceived of as a mechanism that the centre needed to ensure their intentions were implemented, given no power of implementation. This ignores, however, the very real contribution of such techniques to service developments themselves. It was somehow assumed that the role of the centre was value-added and strategic in nature, but working that out in everyday terms was difficult.

For those on the periphery, decentralisation was all too often experienced not as gaining control but as being dumped on. From the periphery it was hard to find connections between budget delegation, new legislation and the operation of demands of increasingly vociferous professional practitioners, local politicians and users.

Much of the change was long overdue. Chapter 4 catalogued the creation of a public service system overweight with a heritage of incremental municipal and professional bureaucracy, unable now to respond in a rapidly changing environment. But one of the characteristics of major organisational changes is that it is always experienced personally and individually. It is experienced as change of personnel, change of job or work organisation and change in responsibilities. And so, though it is irrational, people always imagine that they are the only ones experiencing change; the only ones in stress and, too often, in distress. It is this personal aspect to organisational change that in turn fractures established relationships, disaggregating the corporate change into an atomised and apparently discrete set of situations affecting individuals in their individual ways, some creatively and others not. And it is for this reason that the set of organisational changes pioneered by Thatcher, but not hers alone, have not often been viewed as a whole. For is not our own service special, our own professional contribution singular, and our personal distress strictly personal?

An holistic view of those changes is rather different, suggesting that management techniques were simply the mechanisms to try to bring political control back into a central government struggling with runaway forms of local democracy and overspending.

REVISED FINANCIAL AND POLITICAL ACCOUNTABILITIES

The nature of accountability, between service funder and politician, between professional and manager, between user and provider, depends on three factors. It depends on who is being called to account; for what they are being held accountable; and what form that accountability takes. The changes in public service organizations over the Thatcher era represented changes in all three areas. It was politicians, professionals and managers who were now each being called to account; they were being held accountable politically, professionally and financially, and the form accountability was to take was increasingly modelled on private sector business.

John Stewart and his colleagues (1988) argued that management in the public domain was a more complex process than that of private sector industry. It was concerned with satisficing (i.e. combining satisfaction with optimal solution) rather than optimising. It was about balancing the competing objectives between various stakeholders and moving forward within that frame. Certainly the argument seemed plausible, and sustained a view of management in the public service sector that, for the 1970s and early 1980s at least, was proud of its difference, proud of its special challenge.

Thatcherism would have none of it. Competing objectives and competing stakeholders meant less efficiency. If the objectives could not be resolved, then the answer must be to cut out competing stakes. And this is exactly what happened during the late 1980s with the replacement of political public sector models of accountability with those of the private sector company. This reached its peak with the NHS Reforms, which created a Management Executive and separated purchasers from providers in a top-down heavily managed system. Arguably Thatcherism was right. Low polls at local ballot boxes suggested that traditional forms of public representation were not widely owned, the public preferring to campaign direct if required to do so.

Overall three kinds of changes took place. First, there were changes in the way work was conceived and therefore organised; second there was the rise in managerialism over professionalism; and third there were changes in public representation.

The first set of changes are associated with the cult of consumerism. It was assumed that the use of private sector models would result, if not in consumer sovereignty, as least in consumer orientation. In other words, it was not any business model, but a liberal-pluralist business model which was imported into public service. This expressed itself in a wave of customer-first training, complaints procedures and consumer surveys, amongst other initiatives. This movement, political in origin, had to do with disempowering professionals and must be sharply distinguished from a parallel movement towards user empowerment (see chapter 1). Indeed some argue that consumerism in this form was subsumed by those very professionals it sought to disempower; it was itself 'professionalised', through mechanisms like cooption and tokenism, for example in membership of Community Health Councils and School Governing

Boards. (This argument fails to acknowledge that effective membership, however taken, depends on the member as well as the structure of involvement.)

Work was reorganised to demonstrate value for money, though this concept increasingly gave way in the early 1990s to that of quality. Though the language was different, the idea was much the same. There was a particular construction put on the meaning of quality (James, 1992).

The rise of managerialism over and above professionalism altered accountabilities still further. Some of the rise was explicit, such as in Charles Handy's (1987) *The Making of Managers*, which compared UK management training unfavourably with that in the rest of Europe. The Management Charter Initiative, which grew out of Handy, was ironic in that it sought to give managerialism professional status in its own right at a time when professional status was itself in decline.

But again, it was not just any kind of managerialism that was promoted. It came in industrial Tayloresque form (chapter 4). It said that everybody needed to be managed for the good of the organisation and for the efficient delivery of the product. It said that managers came in three shapes and sizes. There were first-line managers who were basically staff supervisors. There were middle managers who were operational heads and preferably generalists (viz NHS General Managers). And then there were senior managers, who were few in number, situated centrally, and were above all, strategic thinkers (chapter 1). These distinctions were most explicit in the NHS Reforms.

Finally, looking at public representation, this had traditionally taken the form of electoral representation onto a committee, such as the local authority committee. This was to be increasingly replaced by alternative forms of selection and from a different, though equally restricted, choice of candidates. Captains of industry and local business people were to join the newly emerging NHS trust boards as non-executive members. Probation Committee membership was to be reduced from an average of 50 to 15; it was to be widened to include members outside the magistracy and judiciary, and local authority membership was up for reconsideration.

With public representation imitating boards of share holders in private companies, and with changed membership, it was hoped that accountability would shift away from a political and into a financial paradigm and consensus might therefore be possible. Evaluation of achievement of policies, always unsatisfactorily accomplished in committee, would now be revisited in published Annual Reports and against quality assurance measures. Arguably the professional and the committee member swapped roles. The professional gave up the role of rationing to the committee member and argued instead as an advocate of the individual user. Both gave authority to the manager to manage the process. In reality, though services were privatised (e.g. water, electricity) they remained in the public domain in all but financial ways.

The relative ease with which private sector models were assimilated into public service has to be questioned. Certainly public service was unprepared for demonstration of their achievements, based as it was on political rather than information-led decision making. But the nature of many public services and utilities (health, housing, education) were such that they were, as it were, taken for granted. There was no latent or overt aggressiveness which is arguably an attribute of a market-oriented organisation. Faced with that aggressiveness, there was much heart-searching and navel gazing, but very little real construction of an alternative vision.

Success in achieving revised accountabilities was variable depending upon the capacity of government to influence the chosen service. In the NHS it was relatively easy. A Chief Executive was created to head up a clear line management structure. The post was a civil service post, and therefore was directly accountable to the spending department (Department of Health).

It was much harder to call local authorities to account. First there was nobody who could be called to account other than for rare and specific activities (such as the Director of Social Services in cases of child abuse). Then again, local authorities crossed central spending departments, including Environment, Health, and Education and so were able to exploit or blame lack of co-ordinated central direction (e.g. as lead authorities for Community Care implementation).

Tapering, ratecapping and even community tax capping still failed to bring some authorities to task and the government began to look for resolutions that were 'non-political' in character (i.e. not overtly electoral issues). These included returning dependency to the family, to the community or to the workplace, and seeking private sector partnerships. For example 18–21-year-olds dependent on state benefit were returned to dependency on family income and thereby removed from the 'public burden' at a stroke. Crime was to be tackled by 'Safer Cities' and Neighbourhood Watch Schemes, implying a spirit of community living. In this situation, it was assumed, 'local heroes' would emerge, a concept arguably closer to TV soap than to management practice in the 1980s.

In the event private sector sponsorship was not forthcoming on the level anticipated, as evidenced by the much publicised failure to fund the Community Technology Colleges, and the Channel Tunnel financial fiasco.

CONCLUSION

This chapter has argued that the changes demanded of the public sector in the Thatcher era were driven primarily by political will and ideology, though this frequently took its shape from severe resource constraint. It has pointed out most especially three kinds of changes: in defining public and private agendas, in local–central relations, and in revised financial and political accountabilities.

It is important to separate the ideology of the Thatcher years from the set of management techniques brought in during the 1980s to manage the change process. In particular, rejection or acceptance of the one should not unduly influence the other. What the decade illustrates more than anything else is experimentation with management techniques which were quite extraordinary for their range and speed of implementation. Evaluation of them is as yet premature, but they undoubtedly enabled other more advanced forms of organisational design to emerge, and as such acted as a bridge between heavy bureaucratic forms of service delivery and a social market in health and social care.

This argument is developed further in the following chapter, which enlarges the scope of the debate to see organisational shifts in behaviour as triggered, but not caused, by the Thatcher reforms. It seeks to set organisational responses to the Thatcher years within a broader transition including that of management theory and organisational design for a post-Fordist era.

REFERENCES

Audit Commission (1986), *Making a Reality of Community Care*, London: HMSO

Handy, C. (1987), *The Making of Managers: report on the management education, training and development in the USA, West Germany, France, Japan and the UK*, National Economic Development Office

James, A. (1992), Quality and it's social construction by managers in care and service organisations in Kelly, D. and Warr, B. (eds) (1992) *Quality counts: achieving quality in social care organisations*, London: Whiting and Birch Ltd

Home Office (1992), *Partnership in Dealing with Offenders in the community: A Decision Document*

Home Office (1990) *Supervision and Punishment in the Community: A Framework for Action*, CMND 966, London: HMSO

Home Office (1991), *Organising Supervision and Punishment in the Community: A decision document*, London: HMSO

Stewart, J. and Ranson, S. (1988), 'Management of the public domain', *Public Money and Management*, Spring/Summer, vol 8 nos 1 and 2, pp. 13–19

CHAPTER SIX

Managerial responses in the 1980s and 1990s

SUMMARY AND INTRODUCTION

Thatcher's attempts to reform public services produced a number of responses from managers in those services. Of the responses three stand out for their repeated use as mechanisms or even solutions to deal with the rapidly changing world of the 1980s. They were the business solution, the restructuring solution and the planning solution. This chapter looks critically at each of these solutions in turn, regarding them as ways of managing the juxtaposition of large bureaucratic forms of service delivery designed for collective decision making within Thatcher's market-driven system and ideology. It closes by setting these responses within the major contemporary debate within management theory on the nature of strategy.

THE BUSINESS SOLUTION

The business solution was essentially a financially driven solution. It said that successful management depended on successful money management. And of course, at one level it was absolutely right. Doing business had to depend on staying in business. Runaway local budgets meant runaway public expenditure. Both meant political as well as economic suicide for a government and an economy trying to pull itself out of recession.

However, the particular form of business solution which emerged had four assumptions

- that the market would make decisions about health and public welfare, and that the best organisations would survive that process;
- that private sector organisations were more effective than public sector organisations at what they did and how they did it;
- that financial accountability is primary;
- that business decisions are rational and management driven.

The first assumption was based on Thatcher's view that market decisions are simply a collection of individual market transactions between the purchaser (or commissioner) and provider. In this view organisations which are sufficiently customer-conscious will survive.

This view was helpful to public service organisations in persuading them to shift from services designed to serve staff to services designed to serve users. The point was neatly made by Barnardos, who sought to turn themselves from a social work organisation into a child care organisation.

It was nonetheless inadequate to explain the decision-making processes required to manage services for and on behalf of others. Unlike private sector companies (assumption two), public authorities have responsibilities other than to respond to public voice. These include responsibilities to reluctant users (as in the criminal justice system and in statutory child care) and to users often unable or unwilling to express preference to potentially controlling and large bureaucracies without considerable encouragement and the development of self-advocacy skills. These are the sick, the bereaved, people with learning difficulties and with chronic disabilities. Until and unless a certain level and choice of provision can be achieved such that these users can vote with their feet, some decisions over rationing and provision have to continue to be made on behalf of them with their carers and having regard to competing demands from others, including non-users and potential users. Public authorities are forced to make choices between the heard and the unheard, the seen and the unseen. They have to make choices of quality between coverage and depth of service. That is not to discount progressive moves to enhance user empowerment, including the Citizens Charter, but simply to acknowledge the state of the art.

For the relationship between the provider and user is different in a public service agency. In a free market the customer has a choice whether or not to purchase from a given supplier, given limitations of price, proximity, availability and habit. That choice is essentially a business choice. But the relationship of the service user with the service provider is multi-faceted. It is at one and the same time a political relationship (mandated by a vote), a financial relationship (based on payment of a local

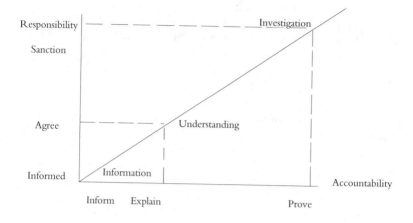

Figure 6.1 Accountability – responsibility relationships in changing committee structures

and national tax) and a dependent or at least unequal relationship (based on the client and the professional).

It is, moreover, not the market itself which facilitates shifts in supply and demand, but the presence and location of money in that market. The issue was not 'how do we free up the market in care services?' but 'where and how should money be invested in the market to promote and sanction and provide incentives?' For the market simply follows money. With the purchaser–provider split completed in the NHS, the issue of 'managing the market' quickly emerged as problematic.

The real advantage of the business model is not therefore in the model itself, but in sharpening up the nature of accountabilities between user, provider and commissioner. It asks what kind of processes do organisations need in order to deliver multiple accountabilities to users, to communities, to professionals, to politicians and to funders.

Looked at in this way the business plan or the community care plan or the delegated budget is a way of demonstrating financial accountability, but only one of a series of processes to ensure accountability for the behaviour of the organisation as a whole. Others include job descriptions and appraisals for staff, quality assurance and inspection for services.

The changing role of public accountability is demonstrated in the reorganisation of the committee (the Probation Committee, the Social Services Committee and the Health Authority Committee). Figure 6.1 demonstrates this.

In its most extreme form, the accounting body (the committee) carries sanctions which can be enforced to require the accountee to prove performance through a process(es) of investigation. At the other extreme the accountee is required simply to inform the accounting body and to acknowledge receipt of information. Between these two accountability/ responsibility relationships lies a third, where the accountee is required to explain and the accounting body to understand and agree.

As financial accountability has become dominant due to pressure on resources and improved capacity to measure efficiency through information technology, so the accountability–responsibility relationship between accounting body and accountee has shifted towards one of sanctions and proof through investigation. Changes to membership of the accounting body to include 'captains of industry' and local figures, often in non-executive roles, has exacerbated this trend. This has given the illusion of a committee that begins to look like a board of shareholders. In fact it is much more complex. Financial accountability is primary to the relationship between the accountee and the accounting body in the board of shareholders. In public service, or in private service which take on the role of public service, accountability is multi-dimensional; the task becomes one of balancing those accountabilities and therefore takes multiple forms, as shown in Figure 6.2.

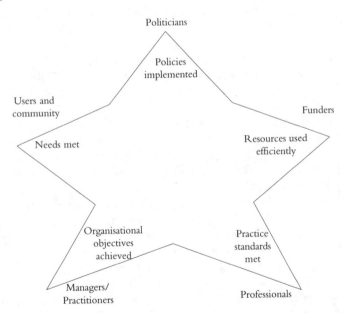

Figure 6.2 Stakeholders and multiple accountabilities in public service

There is accountability to users to meet identified need, to politicians to secure implementation of their policy decisions, to professionals to enable them to practice effectively, to managers to ensure that organisational objectives are achieved, and of course, to funders, to ensure that resources are used effectively.

The need in the 1980s was not to enhance financial accountability, the ethic of which has always been strong in public service, but rather to utilise techniques to demonstrate and sharpen up the practices of financial accountability within a wider remit of these other accountabilities.

The business plan emerged as one way to achieve this. At best the plan forced into the open the need for unit costing and other financial mechanisms required to demonstrate achievement against intention. At worst it was an exercise in flag-waving, designed to demonstrate managerial control in an uncertain environment.

For the business solution promoted under Thatcherism was not any kind of business solution, but one of a certain kind and age. It was based on the rational planning model of Taylorism (chapter 4), now reused and captured for the public sector in the form of management by objectives. It is most clearly seen in the Prison Service, the Probation Service and the Health Service, all of which went through extensive management by objectives (MBO) exercises.

As might be expected, the model did not sit comfortably on organisations designed not to achieve top-down consensus management but to satisfy complex and interactive relationships between competing stakeholders. For some, as in the NHS, the response was to retreat into further rationality in the form of still further planning requirements. Meanwhile private sector industry was dropping MBO in favour of human resource development and issue management, both designed to suit increasingly uncertain environments.

Getting the bottom line right or maintaining financial accountability and credibility is important in order to stay in business. But staying in business is not the same as doing the business. Human services organisations are in business not to stay in business, but to undertake the provision and procurement of human services. The problem with the business solution is that achieving the business plan can become not the process for achieving the goals of the organisation but the goal in itself. Public service organisations had to learn how to sharpen up financial accountabilities to bring them in line with their core mission, not, as with private sector organisations, adapt their core mission to bring it in line with financial advantage.

THE RESTRUCTURING SOLUTION

At one level the whole of Thatcher's revolution of the public service sector can be described as restructuring, using the mechanisms of legislation and policy guidance as key instruments. At another, restructuring was only part of a process of disintegration and reconstruction appropriate to an era of post-Fordism (chapter 4), one running simultaneously through organisations, through nations and even through continents (such as Western and Eastern Europe).

At the organisational level, new structures, both within and beyond the public sector, had three major characteristics. First they were less hierarchical in character. Whole levels of staffing were swept away to leave the three-core strata of strategic, operational and supervisory management. Organisations became less clearly segmented, with responsibilities spread across divisional or departmental structures (e.g. quality assurance). Some segments were removed altogether, most particularly those with specialist technical expertise (such as legal departments or information technology). Instead these skills were bought in as and when required, often in the form of expert consultancy.

Second, structures became leaner and tighter. With a reduction in hierarchical levels and the export of some specialist functions, staff numbers were reduced. As jobs broadened in scope to make up for the shrinkage, accountabilities and responsibilities became much more tightly defined using job descriptions, job appraisals and performance contracts.

The effect of these two characteristics together was to create flatter and smaller core structures with a necessary range of complex relationships with other organisations. The exporting of technical services and the reduction of levels in the hierarchy meant less slack in the system, and with it less capacity to absorb shock. Technical and support services such as training and personnel had worked across divisions and departments often spreading news, information and ideas. Shrinking them or even replacing them with expert consultants reduced the number of such 'mixers and fixers' and unintentionally promoted existing competition, or indeed confrontation, between remaining groups. Moreover, the buying in of expertise substituted a financial relationship for a mutual obligation. At the same time, improved technology meant that work could take place in a number of separate but linked geographical locations. Managing staff was stretched to cover 'second hand' management, that is management of consultants, management by delegation at distance, and management of those not directly or fully employed by the host organisation. This kind of management did not sit easily with the strictly hierarchical distinction between strategic, operational and supervisory management. The effect was to put overload on the middle manager, since the responsibilities of the top manager and the first-line manager could more easily be delineated and therefore defended.

Third, and finally, the new structures were driven by managerial rather than professional processes. Professional structures begin from an assumption that the professional knows best, and that the organisation exists to service that expertise. Professionalism is, moreover, individualistic in character: people become professionals as a result of individual progress through a recognised series of steps which are validated outside the place of work. Loyalty is first of all to the profession and only secondly to the place of work. Transferability between organisations is not only possible, but highly desirable in career terms. Then again, the professional claims a distinctive relationship with the user who is therefore described as a client. And clients attach themselves to individual professionals in preference to an organisation. Management in the professional organisation is a process of trying to bring about order out of a range of individual decisions and activities which taken separately make sense, but taken together may bring about competition or even conflict.

In contrast, structures driven by managers are top-down in that they assume that the best decision is made at the top. The intention is to have that decision owned throughout and a range of control, information and consultation mechanisms are used to try to achieve that. Once decisions are made, control mechanisms come in to ensure those decisions are implemented, as shown in Figure 6.3. Accountability is first of all to the organisation, secondly to the product or service and only thirdly to the customer.

There is inherent tension between the managerial and professional approaches (see Figure 6.4). Large bureaucratic organisations have resolved this tension usually by running the two systems in tandem. In Social Services departments, for example, finance and administration have traditionally been run with a managerial approach, operations with a professional one. This distinction explains the 'them and us' distinction usually found in such organisations. The tandem system usually works reasonably well as long as the two systems are clear about joint outcomes for the organisation as a whole and both are able to maintain a degree of separateness. The effect of reducing the hierarchy and making organisations leaner and tighter is of course to force closer collaboration between the two systems. The outcome is to expose the inherent tension between them and, if irresolvable, to create chaos. In public service organisations, conflict between managerial and professional authority has been most clearly seen in the Health Service, where the drive for general management in the 1980s was powerfully resisted by clinicians.

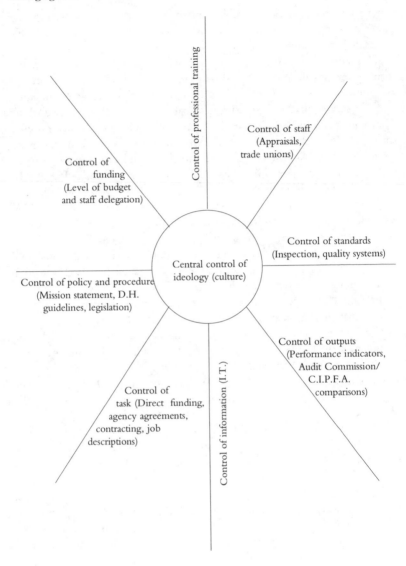

Figure 6.3 Techniques of managerial control in organisations

These three characteristics of the new structures (reduction in hierarchy, leaner and tighter, managerial rather than professional) were expressed in particular ways in the public service organisations of the 1980s. First, they affected relations between the centre (or the headquarters) and the locality. Second they challenged the nature and form of leadership. Third they created more disaggregated and dispersed organisations.

Initially, local structures were miniatures of central structures, like outposts of colonialism. The central structure usually represented the location where the organisation first began, and was therefore itself operational in character. The advent of strategic management together with the potential for distance management brought about by information technology, drew headquarters into a different role. This was to lead a group of local operational units to achieve prescribed organisational objectives. In the private sector this shift of role became most obvious when headquarters moved to the capital or to a regional centre.

In the 1970s, decentralisation programmes had found general support from politicians, professionals and managers in the public service sector. Increasing bureaucratisation of the centre had become stifling of individual initiative, was unnecessarily expensive and arguably not in the interests of users. With caring now the responsibility of the community and of the family in the community, professional ethic combined with political will and financial imperative to dismantle the heavy machinery of central control of welfare in both central and local government.

From a managerial perspective, decentralisation was to be achieved through delegated responsibility for budget and staffing in return for accountability for agreed targets, including financial targets. This process of management required the introduction of a number of mechanisms new to the public service sector, including business planning, performance contracts and quality assurance. These are summarised in Figure 6.3. These mechanisms were adopted to take account of the complex and often competing objectives and particular culture of the public service sector. The pace of change meant that the learning process for using these mechanisms was foreshortened. It was also, in the nature of organisational learning, disjointed, with some parts of organisations ahead of others.

Beneath the language of business were changing relationships around accountability, responsibility and authority. Negotiations between centre and locality were essentially redefinitions of power relationships around control and around the nature and location of community interest. Changing these relationships, as might be expected, had a destabilising effect. While the centre felt they were losing power and authority, the locality often experienced gaining power as increasing their own

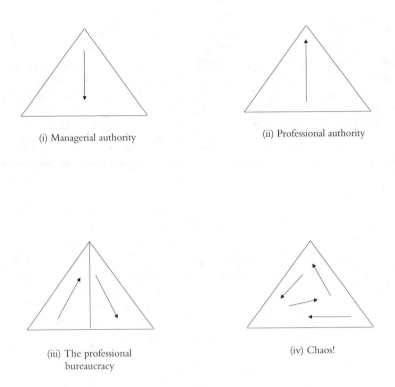

(i) Managerial authority

(ii) Professional authority

(iii) The professional
bureaucracy

(iv) Chaos!

Figure 6.4 Organisational approaches to decision making and authority

uncertainty, and even as dumping by the centre. It was difficult for the centre to recognise what management in the community looked like, and difficult for community management to articulate a process still under formation (chapter 7) and partially invisible. One outcome was to try to push locality management into patterns already tried and tested and therefore to reproduce variations on institutional patterns of care, albeit renamed (e.g. polyclinics).

With hindsight, the unfolding of the change process was bound to be intermittent, incomplete and therefore uncertain. At the time it was experienced as cumulative stress across public service organisations. One response to this stress was to put pressure on leaders of organisations to take on a more directive and upfront role than had traditionally been the case. When times are difficult and situations complex and uncertain, people look for vision, they look for charisma, and they look for authority. Margaret Thatcher was a strong role model. The shift to managerial rather than professional authority brought with it an emphasis on leadership from the top. Titles began to change from chief officers to chief executives in recognition of this shift.

With hindsight, many perceived leaders were less visionary than was perceived at the time. For many vision was simply pulling rank with charisma. Indeed the drive towards what came increasingly to be called 'machismo management' sat uneasily on a public service culture where politicians lead and managers implement. Top managers were unsure how to behave. Some directors of Social Services were sacked or resigned. In their absence, jobs were revised and some were replaced by new posts either of lower rank or combined with other services such as housing. Such revision suited a restrictive financial climate. The Health Service responded by creating general managers and later chief executives in imitation of the private sector, and in recognition of their changing status from administrator to manager to leader.

Decentralisation and changes in the nature of leadership continued to promote the disaggregation of the large bureaucracy. With budgets and staffing responsibilities delegated, decentralised units tended to look to local communities and local organisations to get things done rather than to the centre. To them the role of the centre became less one of adding value than of adding bureaucracy. The opting out of schools from local authority control exemplifies the process. Once responsible for their own budgets and staffing establishments, schools had little remaining use for local education authorities. Their standards were, after all, set not by the education authority, but by the national curriculum operating from Whitehall.

One by one the public services created a language and then a set of mechanisms for disaggregation and dispersal, helped on, and in some services driven, by legislation. Social Services talked about 'commissioning' in a 'mixed economy of care'; local authorities talked of the 'enabling' authority; the Probation Service used the term 'partnership' to describe their new relations with the private and voluntary sectors; the Health Service split into 'purchasers' or 'providers'. The emphasis was on effective joint working, and the intention one of creating a 'seamless service' for users.

One of the main outcomes of the major restructuring that took place in the 1980s and early 1990s was confusion and stress, engendered by the destabilising effect of constant restructuring and with it a concentration on survival as the primary aim. Unable to grasp either an end-view of the changes or sufficient training and support to see them through, some retreated, and left the public service sector. Others became careerist.

Redundancy packages worked in the favour of older staff, but their subsequent absence from the workforce meant a loss of wisdom and was destabilising for new staff. As bureaucratic processes creaked and groaned, staff needed to rely more and more on informal networks for communication and support. In new structures these were sadly lacking. The problem was seen by some as role confusion. If only responsibilities for task could be clarified down and across line management and accountabilities matched, then all would be well. With hindsight, it was in fact the fudging of responsibilities and accountabilities that allowed the new structures, which had after all been artificially imposed, to settle and adapt.

In fact, restructuring of public services away from centralist bureaucracies was vital to survival and to effective service provision in the changing environment. Traditional divisional and departmental structures around specified tasks had suited the bureaucratic requirements of large organisations. The division of labour, line management and job specification had suited a world built for stability, predictability and permanence. In an uncertain world survival would come not from internal bureaucratic processes, but from ability to respond quickly and with flexibility to the world outside. Better to invest in spheres of influence around organisations than levels of authority within it. Better to reorganise tasks for what they are: clusters of actions across organisations, and not discrete activities. Better to recognise level as a function of status, not of management. Better to invest in developing staff than developing structure. In other words, better to recognise that policy making and policy implementation goes on at all levels in the organisation, and organise that process to achieve desired outcomes rather than to allocate responsibilities according to formal structure.

THE PLANNING SOLUTION

In the old days of public service, to manage was the same as to administrate. Chief executives were called general secretaries or chief officers or chief administrators. In the 1960s to manage was not only to administrate but to plan. This was a decade devoted to planning, from housing estates to transport systems, from five-year plans to company strategies.

The notion of strategy, borrowed from the battlefield, like much of the early language of management, still retained something of its military heritage. It suggested that somebody, somewhere, and usually at the top, has a grand organising plan to mobilise resources effectively within a framework of time and place to achieve success.

Popularised in management by Chandler (1962), the term 'strategy' has since taken on a life of its own. In the US the focus was on corporate strategy (known as corporate planning in the UK). In a world characterised by mergers, takeovers and buyouts, corporate strategy was a way of making sense of otherwise separate but conglomerated businesses from the inside. It was, in other words, a way of planning, a way of thinking about a multi-dimensional organisation in the America of the 1960s and early 1970s.

In the UK the term took on rather a different meaning. Less an internal than an external mechanism, strategy described the way in which an organisation managed its environment. Without strategy to ensure its relevance to its environment, an organisation could not remain 'healthy' in the organic, adaptive sense. That did not mean that strategy needed to be explicit, indeed for some it became obvious only with hindsight.

Empirical evidence suggests that strategy is a multi-dimensional term which includes both internal plans and images of the organisation and ways of relating that to the outside world. In fact organisations have many strategies about many aspects of themselves and their critical environments and these operate both formally and informally at a number of levels. Some of them are written up explicitly in the form of business plans or policy and procedural guides. Others of them are implementation techniques passed on and learned informally through staff contact. In fact Tom Evans (1986) makes this explicit when he talks about the 'strands of strategic management' as environmental strategy, substantive (task) strategy, organisational strategy, managerial strategy and change strategy.

So what is the difference between a strategy, a plan, a set of objectives and a policy? The short answer is that we don't know: the language of management is still evolving and people tend to use different words differently. What can be identified however are three broad usages of the term strategy in practice.

For some, strategy is something that you do, that is, it describes the task of the organisation. That task can then be broken down if preferred, in classical MBO style, into sets of objectives. For example in September 1987 the British Institute of Management (BIM) issued what is called a 'Strategy Statement'. This described what the BIM called its 'mission', together with a set of programmes or broad objectives through which it would aim to achieve its mission, a set of activities intended to demonstrate implementation of its objectives or target achievement, and a way of mobilizing its resources. The Statement is reproduced in full in Figure 6.5.

Mission

The mission of BIM is to ensure that the role and importance of management and management development are fully understood, and to help managers and managements achieve the highest professional standards of competence, quality and performance.

Programmes

In furtherance of its mission BIM will:

- Promote broader education for managers;
- Create and deliver education and development programmes aimed at the individual manager and the management team;
- Update and provide information and guidance to its individual members and subscribing organisations;
- Act as the authoritative voice of managers and management on topics of national significance; champion and support enterprise, innovation, the beneficial application of technology, and the creation of wealth in all sectors of the economy.

In support of its programmes BIM will:

- Organise courses, seminars, conferences, working groups and forums;
- Complement its training courses with new distance learning programmes;
- Develop the Management Information Centre as a national resource;
- Utilise electronic and other media in its communications;
- Explain its role as a publisher;
- Stimulate the interchange of management ideas and experience through its branch and regional structure;
- Draw on the skills of its members to the general benefit;
- Work constructively with other institutions and bodies active in its field;
- Participate actively in the media and in public debate.

Resources

BIM will supplement its resources by:

- Stimulating use of its educational and information services;
- Seeking sponsorship and other financial support for particular programmes and activities;
- Concluding arrangements where appropriate.

Figure 6.5   BIM Strategy Statement (Source: *Management News*, September 1987)

For others, strategy is something you think. It is the principle of the organisation, its mind set and its approach. For example the ways in which British Airways began to change their organisation came out of a view that British Airways is in a business not about aircraft but about passengers. So an organisation that had started as an aircraft industry using wartime planes and wartime pilots had to rethink itself into a customer-centred service organisation.

A third view of strategy, and the one with perhaps most mileage, is that strategy is both a way of thinking about the organisation (i.e. who we are) and a set of activities to deliver the business of the organisation (i.e. what we do) and more besides: it is also a way of behaving. In other words the way an organisation does its business is as important as the business it does. This view says that identifying a vision is important; identifying a set of activities designed to achieve that vision and ways of measuring achievement is also important. However, that vision will not be achieved through those tasks without attention to organisational process.

This view leads us to think very differently about strategy, about planning and about the job of management. In the 1960s, planning and administration might well have been the same as managing. With resource capability and an environment which welcomed change for the better, it was perfectly possible to set a goal, plan a strategy, implement and review it, as Figure 6.6 illustrates.

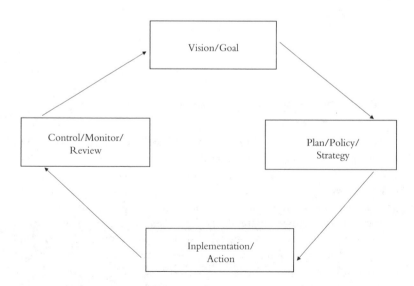

Figure 6.6 The planning cycle (1960s)

The new world works rather differently. Managers still produce plans; they still try to implement them and review them against overall vision. The difference is that they very rarely get to complete this process before the world has changed again, requiring a different kind of plan. Indeed plans often get stuck much earlier, at the implementation stage.

In contrast, if we consider what managers actually do, as opposed to what the planning process tells them to do, we find something rather different going on. Managers tend to act first; review their action; look for patterns and themes in their actions that might, in hindsight, be called a strategy, and finally measure up the outcomes of the strategy against the vision (see Figure 6.7). This rather different order of events does not mean managers are managing badly; it simply means that the planning process cannot keep up with the changing demands on the manager.

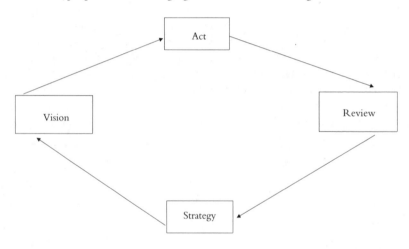

*Figure 6.*7   The management implementation cycle (1990s)

When we begin to examine the difference between planning and management, we begin to understand something of the difference between the two processes. Stages identified in the planning process (vision, strategy, implementation, review) are public activities designed to demonstrate and win ownership. They are the shop window of the business of management. Behind the shop window is the real business of management: diagnosing capability, building relationships, listening and giving feedback and taking learning back into a re-evaluated vision (Figure 6.8 demonstrates).

In the new world of management, the distinction between public and private, between planning and management, remains, though the processes

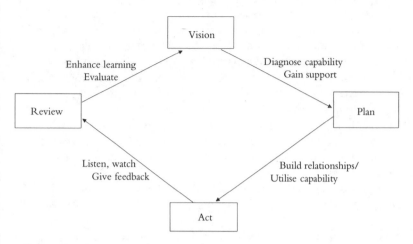

Figure 6.8 Management planning cycle

are rather different. So the manager who acts 'on the hoof' has then to buy off dissatisfaction with their action, to review and learn from it, then institutionalise that learning through a strategy which suits the vision. The manager's action is informed by key priorities arising out of the vision. The process is therefore iterative (see Figure 6.9).

Distinguishing planning from the business of management is not to say that planning is not important to the management process. Policy makers

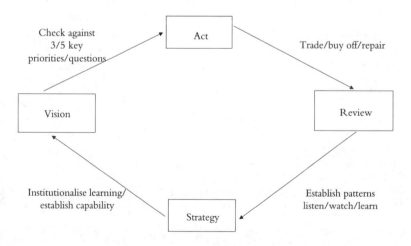

Figure 6.9 Management implementation cycle

need plans, as do financiers and organisations. The difference is that the managers need to be able to implement plans as well as construct them. In order to do that they need to be able to distinguish between a plan designed for a specific audience or purpose, and a working plan for themselves. In other words they need to be able to operate front stage and back stage. They need to know that while route-plans for public consumption follow a formal structure (Figure 6.5), that structure does not necessarily match up in real life. If they fail to make this distinction, they continue to believe the myth that if only they worked harder, faster or trained more thoroughly, they would be able to implement the formal plan successfully.

The problem is a particularly difficult one for managers since their jobs require them to feed into a planning process which is usually centrally determined. Central government departments are accustomed to presenting policy intentions in the form of plans, and of measuring achievement against plan. Local organisations appear to have replicated this process and not to have distinguished the needs of the policy makers from the behaviour of managers. Some managers appear to have done the same.

THE CONTRIBUTION OF STRATEGY

To apply this now to our earlier discussion on strategy: what we have in summary are three different usages of the term. Strategy is what we do, why we do it, and how we do it. And of course strategy might be any one combination of these three. This empirical observation is backed up by theoretical analysis, which in turn identifies three major approaches.

The rational approach

What I have called the rational approach to strategy are those methods and techniques based essentially on forward planning. Located initially in militarism, the forward planning model became dominant during and after the Second World War not only as a way of running a business, but also as a way of administering public services. As chapter 4 demonstrates, the creation of the welfare state was predicated on a particular view of how services were to be delivered using a combination of municipal socialism, industrial organisation and bureaucracy.

Applied to strategy, the model is based on five assumptions. First, it assumes that decisions can be planned in advance. We are talking, in other words, about a world that will wait for a decision, whereas the reality of managing in the 1990s is that some decisions must be made immediately and justified afterwards. The difference has been popularised, again in military terms, as 'fire, steady, aim'. Second, it assumes that the best decisions are those which are best informed, and therefore tremendous effort is put into improving the collection, analysis and dissemination of information. It assumes conversely that bad decisions must have been badly informed. Yet again the evidence is that strategic management decisions are made less on the basis of information than on information combined with opportunity and 'gut feeling' or instinct. Third, it assumes that decisions are made top-down and implementation is cascaded through the hierarchy. In practice much strategic decision making is made 'on the hoof', case by case and is emergent rather than explicit. Fourth, it assumes that information that cannot be coded is extraneous 'noise' or irrelevant, rather than that the process model is inadequate. And finally, it assumes that appeal to reason and intellect will draw a consensus, an assumption that does more than anything else to invalidate the model when measured against experience!

Around the rational model have grown up a range of techniques designed to facilitate an improved planning process. These include very helpful ways of collecting and reordering certain kinds of information, such as environmental context through a PEST analysis (see chapter 2), analysis of the organisation using SWOT (strengths, weaknesses, opportunities, threats), analysis of the critical environment using competitor analysis, and so on. Once reordered a range of techniques are available to determine options and help choose between them, such as decision analysis or critical path analysis, techniques stemming from operations research. Then again these options can be measured against possible future scenarios through other predictive techniques like scenario-building or Delphi judgements.

But if the assumptions underpining the rational model don't measure up to reality, what use can be made of these techniques? Furthermore, if the model is faulty, why is it so well used? The answer is, of course, that the value of the techniques is not only, not even primarily, in the information generated about the business. The value is in the process of organisational learning that takes place among the key participants. The techniques, used carefully, can themselves move on strategic thinking, such that information stops becoming information about what, starts becoming information about why, and ends up, in the best situation at least, becoming information about how.

Why the model itself, though faulty, is so well used is rather more difficult to answer. It is difficult because it raises the notion of what I have called 'as-if management'. If you know what you want to do, don't know how to do, but are invested with the power of knowing, then there is tremendous pressure to operate 'as if' you know. And for many this is exactly what management is. At its worst it represents what has been called 'macho management', which is all display and has become falsely aligned with gender behaviour. As its very best it could represent 'holding the vision' on behalf of an organisation in trauma. Most of the time it is somewhere in between.

The reason why rational strategic models are so well used is because our heritage of industrial planning fits so comfortably with 'as-if management'. Like the emperor without clothes, it is in no one's interest to admit that planning doesn't really work and that managers don't really know how to do things. Better to revise the plan on a regular basis and train the managers to do their job. And this is exactly what happens in practice. And theory is adapted to suggest that even grand strategy is contingent to circumstances of time and place. Planning is combined with 'logical incrementalism' (Quinn 1980) so that the manager 'muddles through' (Lindblom 1959).

The market approach

What I have called the market approach to strategy takes its lead not from behaviour within the organisation but from that in its critical environment. Examples of this approach are the portfolio approach of the Boston Consulting Group and Porter's (1980) traditional competitor analysis. The portfolio approach studies products in relation to market share and market penetration. It suggests that products are either 'stars', 'cash cows', 'dogs' or 'question marks', and every robust company should aim to balance their product range over these groupings. Stars are products with high market share and potential for high market growth (i.e. they are products on the ascent); cash cows are products which are milked to provide finance for question marks (the up-and-coming but as yet new product). Dogs are the products on the way out. The model assumes that products have a life history against which performance can be measured.

Porter's model looks for competitive advantage (that is, a gap in the market) by an analysis of five factors: the relative power of the customer, of the supplier, the threat of substitute products, the threat of new entrants and the levels of competition in the chosen industry.

In contrast Kottler (Kottler and Andreasen 1987), the dominant name in marketing, focuses on the nature of the customer, identifying a group or groups of customers as a target and then marketing a product to hit them. This is the notion of market segmentation and creating a market mix designed to hit several market segments at once.

The market approach to strategy has found increasing support within the public service sector with the introduction of a business culture and the creation of induced market conditions such as competition and contracting out. Indeed John Patten, when Under-Secretary of State at the Home Office spoke to a conference of probation staff at Birmingham University in 1989 suggesting that the Probation Service needed a broader 'market segment' than that of the traditional offender. Moreover, some of the problems of the service, he said, were down to poor marketing and poor self-image.

In practice there are serious problems with the approach. While the implied significance of users, or 'consumers' in this language, is welcomed, there are obvious problems in the wholesale translation of private sector industrial techniques to the public and voluntary service sectors. These have been detailed elsewhere by John Stewart (1986) and others and need not be repeated here.

Of more concern is the level of analysis of the techniques, many of which are simply analogies rather than models or theories. Moreover they are analogies with less credence even in the private sector as time goes by.

Ansoff makes a similar point when he says:

> Just as in the earlier shift from production to the marketing orientation, the shift to a post-industrial orientation is still unrecognised or resisted in many firms because it introduces new uncertainties, threatens a loss of power by the entrenched managers, requires new perceptions and new skills. The resistance to change frequently leads to a gap between the behaviour of a firm and the imperatives of the environment. The firm continues to focus on marketing and disregards the technological and political changes. (Ansoff 1984: p. 6)

Of more relevance is Normann's (1984) service management, another market approach, but this time located in service rather than production. Normann identifies five sets of questions which interrelate to create a service strategy. He asks: what do we do here? (service concept); who is our customer? (market segment); how do we package our service? (service delivery system); what kind of people are we (image or culture); and what is the value-added function of the centre (i.e. what are the incentives in belonging to the centre rather than remaining independent).

Of significance to understanding strategy in service organisations is Normann's view of the customer as intrinsic to the service process, not an optional extra. For him, service starts from within the organisation, not from a product or request for a product, but from what he calls the 'moment of truth'. This is what happens when the client and the service provider meet and together create or do not create either a single transaction or an ongoing relationship. It is the multiplicity of these separate moments of truth that together create momentum for a service delivery system and therefore for an organisation. Each moment of truth ripples to create an holistic approach: small is beautiful is big. This is bottom-up management and genuine consumerism and has much to commend it.

The political approach

The third view of strategy I have called the political approach. This is the view which equates the business of managing with ways of behaving. Put colloquially, 'It's not what you do but the way that you do it', and, not insignificantly, ends, 'that's what gets results'. Political approaches to strategy are represented by contingency theories of management. At its crudest, contingency theory is opportunism; that is, the manager manages according to opportunities presented by what has been termed a 'surpriseful' environment (Heath *et al.*) 1988.

The theory has much to commend it as a way of justifying management practice in a heavily political environment. Crudely, local authority chief officers might use newsworthy information, such as child sexual abuse, increasing crime figures, or lower levels of child literacy, to make a bid for additional resources. The style is not without its problems, for example when bids for professional resources are not backed up by ancillary or administrative staffing costs. It does little either for planning by other staff back home, for whom policy decisions appear at best as accidental, at worst as beyond control. However, it works well for the leader whose capacity to sway political audience is regarded as charismatic.

A more sophisticated version of the theory measures opportunities offered, or indeed potentially created, against the strategic intent of the organisation. In other words opportunities which fit in with the general strategic drive or intention of the organisation are picked up and others are not. The problem of course is that this assumes strategic intent is explicit and indeed, accurate, whereas in practice much that is strategic intent appears so only with hindsight.

The theory is developed more fully with Quinn's 'logical incrementalism' and Lindblom's 'disjointed incrementalism'. Both describe strategy as made up of a series of apparently small but nonetheless irreversible decisions which together incrementally, move the direction of the organisation towards some ends and away from others. Strategy is emergent rather than explicit (Mintzberg 1983).

John Bryson (1988) talks much more overtly about strategy as a political process when he uses the term 'stakeholders' to identify the key players in an organization. For Bryson, strategy is the outcome of interplay between the stakeholders, and strategic management the management of that interplay. Zimmerman (1971) however, alerts us to the notion that the strategy of the organisation is not in fact that of the interplay (it is not 'satisficing' the stakeholders), but rather the view of the dominant group. Clearly there are links here with the notion of hegemony in late Marxism. And of course it rings true empirically that some people's views carry more weight than others.

But perhaps the ultimate political theory of strategy is that often described as Japanese. Caricatured as 'no strategy', it is characterized by Mitsubishi's apparent ability to jump strategies midstream, a facility not without merit in a rapidly changing environment. For success it depends not on making strategy explicit, but on keeping it secret in order to retain competitive edge. It relies on a responsive culture among staff which accepts apparent switches in production activities with confidence. It works by focusing on a link series of priorities known to all staff but identified through the constant use of the same few strategic questions used by senior management at every key decision point.

CONCLUSION

In conclusion, three major responses of public service agencies in the 1980s (the business response; restructuring; planning) can be regarded as attempts to bring organizations into line with a radically changing environment. To that extent they are strategic in nature. Within them we can identify strains of the three major approaches to strategy (rational planning, the market approach, the political approach). What we find is public sector organisations struggling to achieve at the cutting edge of management theory, and indeed challenging some of that theory.

REFERENCES

Ansoff, H.I. and McDonnell, E. (1984), *Implanting Strategic Management*, Englewood Cliffs, NJ: Prentice-Hall

Bryson, J. (1988), *Strategic Planning for Public and Non-profit Organisations*, Jossey-Bass

Chandler, A.J. (1962), *Strategy and Structure: Chapters in the History of the American Industrial Enterprise*, Cambridge, MA: MIT Press

Evans, T. (1986), in *In Dreams begins Responsibility: a tribute to Tomm Evans*, London: King Edward's Hospital Fund for London 1987

Heath, R.L. *et al.* (1988), *Strategic Issues Management*, Jossey-Bass

Kottler, P. and Andreasen, A. (1987), *Strategic Management for Non-profit Organisations*, Englewood Cliffs, NJ: Prentice-Hall

Lindblom, C.E. (1959), 'The science of muddling through', *Public Administration Review*, vol 1, Spring, reproduced in Pugh, D.S. (ed) (1971), *Organisation Theory: selected readings*, London: Penguin

Mintzberg, H. (1983), *Power in and around Organisations*, Englewood Cliffs, NJ: Prentice-Hall

Norman, R. (1984), *Service Management: Strategy and Leadership in Service Businesses*, Chichester: Wiley

Porter, M.E. (1980), *Competitive Strategy; Techniques for Analysing Industries and Competition*, London: Free Press, Macmillan

Quinn, J.B. (1980), *Strategies for Change; Logical Incrementalism*, Illinois: Irwin

Stewart, J. (1986), *Strategic Management in Local Government*, Discussion Paper MS 0067, London: LGMB

Zimmerman, D.H. (1971), 'The practicalities of rule use' in Douglas, J.D. (ed) *Understanding Everyday Life*, London: Routledge & Kegan Paul

CHAPTER SEVEN

Professional bureaucracies, markets and networks: managing beyond the market

SUMMARY

The 1980s have seen a paradigm shift in the construction of public services. We have evolved from a world which regarded stability as the norm and prelearning a necessity, to one which is increasingly uncertain and surpriseful.

Chapter 7 brings together the threads of that shift, and offers a framework for making sense of it, a framework based on professional bureaucracies, market and networks. It argues that the market applied by Thatcher across the range of public services, though it has a very real contribution to make, is inherently flawed as a way of managing public service. It suggests that the model has been overlaid across a receding, but nonetheless entrenched and all-pervading, model of professional bureaucracy. It argues that the agenda for the future is to learn to live with diversity in the construction and delivery of human services and for the co-existence of bureaucratic and market models together with another emerging model, that of networks. It promotes an agenda which pays primary attention to the interface between these diverse ways of working.

Finally it returns to the major theme of the book that managing human services is similar to managing other services, but it is not the same. It is not the same because such services are created on behalf of vulnerable people. The primary task of public services is to represent, to advocate and to empower that group of people within a set of competing political, economic and social choices. This remains the challenge and the conundrum in a post-Thatcher environment.

We live in exciting times. The Berlin Wall has come down and we are watching the violent fracturing of an all-pervading state system in Eastern Europe. This volume has repeatedly drawn connections between major world events and analogous behaviour in the deconstruction and reconstruction of public services (chapters 2 and 4). Not since Beveridge have we seen changes to our health and welfare services on a scale experienced in the 1980s and 1990s. To be an observer of these changes is challenge enough, to be a participant in them a privilege. Thatcher did us two favours. First she triggered a set of changes across the public service sector with a consistency and speed which created the potential for nothing less than a paradigm shift in thinking about the delivery of human services. Second, she left the premiership before an alternative paradigm was in place. As such she was an agent of the transition rather than a harbinger of the future (chapter 1).

The effect of experimentation with a market model has been to open up the debate. That debate is chaotic, in the technical sense of the word. That is, while it experienced as disengaged and confused, it holds within it certain shapes and patterns which already capture what will become the predominant modes of service delivery for the future. Of these two are dominant and arguably a third is emergent: the professional bureaucracy, the market and the network.

THE PROFESSIONAL BUREAUCRACY

Arguably the professional and the bureaucratic are different organisational forms which have been fused in public service through an accident of chronology (chapter 4). Figure 7.1 uses a number of criteria to identify the difference between forms of organisations (perceived nature of the business, the form authority takes, staff relationships and client relationships).

In the professional model the business of the organisation is perceived as being around the person of the professional. In the Health Service we talk of 'going to see the doctor'. For the business is medicine, or doctoring, or clinical practice, or nursing or general practice. In Social Services the business is social work. In education it is teaching. In contrast, in the bureaucratic model, the business is perceived as that which the organisation is seen to deliver, namely public services. So in the Health Service the business is hospitals (we talk of 'going to the hospital'), in education it is schools, in social services it is services for vulnerable groups of people. In the bureaucratic model the visible service is more powerful than the invisible service.

The authority of professionals lies in their expertise. Therefore power in professional organisations becomes associated with the exclusivity and

How organisations work	Professional	Bureaucratic	Business	Network
Organisation				
1 Nature of the business described by	Professional identity	Description of service	Product(s)	Empowerment
2 Source of authority	Expertise	Line, rank	Market share	Capacity to enable
3 Staff relations with management	Consult	Instruct	Negotiate	Exchange
4 User relations	Client	Recipient	Customer	Colleague
5 Interagency relations	Explicit non-competition	Self-sufficiency	Competitive	Collaboration
People				
Leaders	Professionals	Administrators	Entrepreneur/dealer	Multiple leadership
Incentives	Job satisfaction, pride; Uniqueness	Promotion, control over increasing resources	Margins and market share	Robustness
Disincentives	Exclusion, isolation	Resource-freezing or reduction	Risk	Invisibility; Lack of status
Accountability	Professional	Employer	Purchaser	User
Skills predominating	Technical expertise	Compliance	Market sensitivity	Vision, empathy
Environment				
Nature of relationship with colleagues	Co-professional	Line	Contractual	Equal
Nature of regulation	Self-regulating	Political and legal	Legal and commercial	User charters

Figure 7.1 Managing with diversity

elitism born of sophisticated and lengthy induction processes and, as a result, with extensive inter-professional rivalry. Clinical rivalry is a case in point. The bureaucratic form of authority lies in rank and line. So the chief executive in the Health Service or the Local Authority, once removed from office finds himself or herself suddenly without power.

In the professional bureaucracy there is a constant tussle between these two sources of authority. In that tussle the professional has often won, through more effective and consistent coordination of power into professional lobbies, such as the Royal Colleges. Thatcher's denigration of the power of the professional was accompanied by a rise in the power of the administrator turned manager. In consolidating that shift in power, the manager began to claim professional status for management. Sometimes the tussle was resolved by appointing professionals in leadership positions, such as clinical directors in the Health Service. It is not accidental that the trend to appoint directors of Social Services or their equivalent without social work qualification came about in the late 1980s and early 1990s with the emergence of the manager as professional.

If the authority of the professional lies in expertise, then relations with staff reinforce that expertise. Professionals consult with others, including peers, but ultimately make their own decisions, assuming their superior expertise requires them to do so. In a bureaucracy, authority is passed up and down the line, so staff are informed rather than consulted by managers, on the basis that those at the top are paid more to take the harder decisions. This makes for difficulties in the professional bureaucracy, where some staff are consulted and others are informed. Professional decisions are frequently confused with administrative or bureaucratic decisions, not least because they often run across staff working in different modes. The result is that some staff complain that they haven't been consulted; others that people (usually those above them in rank) can't make decisions.

Then again in the professional organisation the user is the client, and a strict relationship is ensured between professional and client such that the professional knows best. In the bureaucracy the user is the recipient of services provided by the organisation. In both models the user is passive and this mutual reinforcement of passivity is one reason why user empowerment cannot be successfully achieved within professional bureaucracies.

So what happens to people who work in professional bureaucracies? Both professional and bureaucratic forms require highly segmented organisational structures. For the professional this means reinforced exclusivity and uniqueness; pride centres around becoming the most exclusive, the most specialist. For bureaucrats too, status is based on promotion, so there is inbuilt reinforcement towards compliance and empire-building. One effect is to create organisations in which people are at worst isolated, at best identify with only a small segment and fail to contribute to the whole.

Clearly these kinds of organisation work best in an environment which is safe and predictable, and which doesn't require people to change their skills or to work across organisational boundaries. Self-regulating professional organisations score on persistence and on resilience to change. In contrast bureaucratic organisations are normally politically regulated. This works well in a politically stable environment. Arguably the demise of the bureaucracy has much to do with political instability.

Certain types of organisations create certain kinds of leaders. The professional organisation puts super-crafts people at its head. So, for example, a large part of the BBC is led by ex-producers. These leaders can carry extensive credibility within the organisation and often great personal authority and even charisma because of their craft. They are, however, an extreme form of functional leader, with achievement dependent on excluding wider views and on making correct decisions. As such they are unlikely to carry the personal skills required of a corporate chief executive to bring different interests together for the effectiveness of the agency as a whole.

THE MARKET ORGANISATION

Using our very crude model (Figure 7.1), in the market organisation the nature of the business is defined by the product or by a collective term which describes the range of products (e.g. Yamaha is in the entertainment and leisure business). Authority is determined by market share and margin. The user is the consumer, and the way business is done is by negotiation rather than by consultation or instruction.

The kind of environment which suits the market organisation is one where purchasers and providers are clearly delineated such that contracts between the two can be negotiated. Regulation is legal and commercial such that organisations not responding to their environment do not survive.

People who flourish in market environments are those able to bring purchasers and providers together in productive ways. Aware of the needs of both, they are traders operating on the edges of their own organisations. They therefore need to be flexible and able to adapt their skills in a rapidly changing environment.

Does the market organisation succeed as a model for delivering health and welfare services? Clearly there is no simple answer. What has happened is that at the highest, and arguably the simplest, strategic levels, the legislative framework has been put in place. Similarly there has been movement, variable according to service, at the professional and practitioner levels of activity. Teachers, doctors, social workers, probation officers and prison officers are designing and participating in new ways of delivering services. Increasingly these involve co-working with other professionals, a wide variety of performance contracts, developing financial accountability and some commitment to enhanced user participation.

What remains uncertain is at the middle level. While the government has spelled out what must happen, and professional practitioners have got on with the everyday interface of service delivery, there remains considerable doubt about how to make the connections between grand strategy and everyday life. There is, for instance, a whole gap in commissioning in the Health Service between spot contracts and block contracts, a whole gap in Social Services between accessing the need of populations in community care plans and implementing individual packages of care.

It is assumed that somehow these gaps will resolve themselves through the activities of the market. So general practitioners in the health market, and housing associations in the housing market, are the loose balls rolling around, and, it is naively assumed, acting as market entrepreneurs to fill the gap. At the same time the government is seen to be getting cold feet over the worse excesses of the market place (e.g. failure to implement in full Tomlinson's report on London's hospitals). Though the rhetoric of managing the market is extensive and growing, there is no clear evidence at date of publication of capacity to exert significant leverage in the system. What there is is evidence of mapping, of spending, of staffing and of populations, whether in business plans, in trust applications or in community care plans. And arguably much of the business of retargeting according to identified need and agreed priorities would have happened anyway (viz Welsh strategy on mental handicap).

THE NETWORK ORGANISATION

The professional bureaucracy is a highly developed and articulated organisational form. The market organisation is less so, certainly in relation to the quasi-market of public service. Both have their strengths and weaknesses. Their overwhelming weakness is their failure to promote the empowerment of users and to be able to make the transfer from directly managed and visible units into indirectly managed and invisible forms of service enablement.

So what kind of organisation might be expected to service communities and assist them in achieving their own image of a healthy community? Certainly not the hierarchical and Tayloresque organisation of the planned economy described as the professional bureaucracy (chapter 3) which separates operation from control and which runs smoothly by cutting out extraneous feedback or noise from the environment. Certainly not the market organisation which seeks to satisfy the purchaser with the biggest bankroll. And yet we went to elaborate lengths to preserve and adapt our hierarchical organisations, as chapter 5 describes, and to enormous trouble to simulate market conditions in public service.

In fact the seeds of these new organisations, like most of the developments which will occur over the next fifteen years, are already with us. Hjern and Porter (1981) get closest to describing them when they talk about 'implementation organisations'. While having some characteristics of both hierarchical and market organisations, implementation organisations are different to both. Like hierarchical organisations they seek to address multiple accountabilities, but no longer through notions of standardisation and uniformity (arguably bureaucratic substitutes for equality), but rather through improved information systems, through quality systems and through published plans and policies. Like market organisations they respond to individual customers and hold members of staff accountable as individuals for performance by a series of incentives and disincentives. They take account of more than customer preference (in Hjern and Porter's terms, they address 'ought as well as want'). They are about more than individual purchaser–provider transactions, but about less than all-pervasiveness. In other words they take account of the network of social obligations and responsibilities that underpin market transactions and which, other than price, determine how we decide with whom we do business and how we conduct that business. Indeed the complexity of the organisation and its multiple accountabilities is a source of strength not weakness. It ensures that commitment is to outcomes and not to employing agencies. It is for this reason that I have called them network organisations.

Examples of the network organisation include some of the company welfare schemes and some examples of good practice in joint agency activity. Many of the preferred company welfare schemes come from Japan and Germany and recognise a reciprocal relationship between employees and their company. Clearly they owe allegiance to a cultural form as yet not articulated in the UK. In contrast some of the US company schemes, which are market rather than company driven, have generated excessive competition among providers and excessive wants as opposed to needs among employees.

The network organisation is not housed in one place, with one set of staff and one budget, but is simply the place where things get done. It is like a project group in that it may be life-limited and outcome-focused, but it is more than a project group in that it is self-accountable and there to implement rather than to plan. It works 'on the hoof'.

The difference between a network implementation organisation and a project group is firstly in the way the group perceives of itself and secondly in the ways it conducts its business. The creation of such implementation organisations is not, as is often assumed, peripheral to the 'real' work of hierarchical institutions. Rather they represent a transition to a different form of organisation and one which takes its legitimacy from the community. If the future of health and welfare is seamless service then separate and hierarchical institutions cannot survive.

To go back to Figure 7.1, the network organisation perceives its business as enabling. So in the Health Service, its business is, in the jargon, 'health gain'. It works by divesting authority in others, by empowerment. It operates on a system not of instruction (bureaucracy), consultation (professionalism) or negotiation (market) but of on-going exchange ('I'll do this for you and you'll do something for someone else'). People who flourish in network organisations are those who can hold onto an image of connectedness without necessarily needing the superstructure of buildings or of professional identity to hold them together. Regulation comes from the user, in the form of quality assurance and participation.

The conception of the network organisation frees us to think differently about existing organisations. Public service no longer needs to correlate with hierarchy. Private no longer needs to be the opposite to public. Pluralism does not have to exclude individual initiative, nor democracy professional discretion. Information about needs of communities no longer needs to be organisationally specific. Indeed organisations can themselves be simply nodules on a network that is itself the community. The paradigm shift is in the mind of the perceiver.

MANAGING DIVERSITY

But if the future of public services is potentially around the network organisation, the past and the present is very much around the professional bureaucracy and the market. To have identified different forms of organisational design is not to say that one is better or worse; only that it may be more or less suitable for the environment in which it has to operate, more or less comfortable for the staff who work in it, and, above all, more or less appropriate for the needs of its service users.

That is not to say that public service is required to move away from professional bureaucracy and into network arrangements. It is rather to recognise the value in the diversity of different management arrangement and different organisational forms both within and across organisations. It is not to argue whether or not the market has replaced the professional bureaucracy or simply overlaid it, but rather to acknowledge the strengths and weaknesses of both. For it may be that certain parts of organisations, or certain kinds of organisation, work more effectively in one mode rather than another. The issue then is one of constructing interfaces.

Joint working and seamless service provision has not worked in the past, not because we have not tried hard enough or worked at it long enough. It hasn't worked because it is predicated on models of organisation – culture, budgets, boundaries, systems, staffing – being sufficiently the same to make it a reality. Once we begin to distinguish between different models, we can begin to design new forms of interaction between them. It may be that crude mechanisms for that interaction should and will persist. This includes mechanisms like joint post-holding, cross-subsidising, joint planning, joint training and a joint language. But the mechanisms will not be ends in themselves but part of an integrated design process for seamless service provision.

At the present time professional bureaucracies, markets and networks sit together uncomfortably. They do so because each tries to communicate with the other by imposing its own mind set. So the market organisation tries to deal with the rest of the system by the use of contracts. For example, the purchaser or the provider in the Health Service deals with the Regional Health Authority and the general practitioner by agreeing a contract. Contracts, however, are not the means of communication of the professional. Traditionally professionals have communicated their intentions through joining together in professional associations. So the professional response to the general practitioner or consultant contract comes from the Royal Colleges. Moreover it utilises a style not of negotiation (the market) but of consultation. Then again the network organisation feels particularly difficult for the professional bureaucracy to work with because it is fluid, largely invisible, and operating on an exchange rather than a command model. So, for example, local authorities find great difficulty securing appropriate accountability from small voluntary organisations and community groups.

In fact what is required is not that one form of organisational design intrudes upon another. Rather that there needs to be clarity about the nature and purpose of the interface and the creation of appropriate mechanisms to achieve that. A colleague, Martin Fisher, talks about 'monoclonal antibodies' and their capacity to change shape in order to connect different surfaces. At a more simplistic level we might think of press-studs or buttons and button holes, where the garment is not intended to be seamless, but where fastenings are specifically designed to interconnect.

Managing leadership in diversity, then, requires two sets of skills. At one level it requires functional leadership of an organisation within its environment: the traditional role of the chief executive. At another meta-level, effective leadership depends on managing the interfaces effectively, and therefore adding value to the public service as a whole. This means managing competing mind sets, different chronologies, separate power bases and above all, managing the fear which underpins the process of transition.

CONCLUSION

This volume has catalogued a chronology of change: change in the political, economic, social and technological context of public services (chapter 2); the thrust of professionalism (chapter 3); and the domination of Taylorsque and bureaucratic forms of service delivery (chapter 4). It has described the Thatcher era (chapter 5) and articulated the three main managerial responses to its demands (chapter 6).

Not unnaturally in the aftermath of Thatcherism we are experiencing a lack of momentum, even a vacuum, in promoting a privatised market in public service. Two explanations are emerging for this.

The first is in the amended language of the social market (Leadbetter 1991), a market principle softened by John Major and William Waldegrave to include the Citizens Charter and to confine the runaway activities of free market providers (e.g. NHS Hospital Trusts and their restrictions on capital borrowing). This includes a rhetoric now surfacing about the inherent value of the public services ethic, a rhetoric which appears to go back to John Major's personal career experiences at Lambeth.

The second is less an explanation than a backlash against the market principle. The break-up of Eastern Europe, initially welcomed as the dawn of new era, is rapidly disintegrating into a bloody power struggle. So the NHS, even as third-wave trusts come on stream, is facing fractured relationships due to the purchaser and provider split, myopia caused by constant and inward-looking planning and restructuring exercises and the repeated blaming of parts of the system not as yet operating within a single and singularly narrow interpretation of the market. There are signs that the government has lost its nerve over the market in health care, for instance on its questioning of capacity to attach real spending to floating a market in primary care in accompaniment to the closure of some of London's key hospitals after the Tomlinson report. This argument, put forward by Osbourne and Gaebler (1992), acknowledges the absence of a new paradigm and looks simply to instances of good practice and successful public services endeavours to capture potential characteristics of precursors to a new paradigm.

But there could be a third explanation. Over the last ten or fifteen years we have been faced with a rhetoric of management that has now disintegrated. As with the economy, in our uncertainty we have experimented with a range of theories and models, and come up with none that is as yet appropriate to our changed situation. So in management we have laboured under a set of theories that have in turn sought to define task (management by objectives); to clarify resources (management of human resources, management by cash limits); to reunite structures, systems and strategies (management by restructuring, management by information technology, management by policy and protocol). Finally we have attempted to change cultures (management by vision and values). (See Figure 4.2.).

The demise of Thatcherism has brought with it the demise of single vision. It is too early to say whether or not Thatcher and her contemporaries, notably Kenneth Clarke in the public sector, were truly visionary or simply forceful and directional personalities. What we do find post-Thatcher is less an absence than a multiplicity of visions for public service as represented in the variety of White Papers emerging in the early 1990s. It is this multiplicity of visions which makes leading organisations in transition such a difficult job to do. It may be that chief executives have to invent visions for the effective coordination of their organisations. It may be that visions never really existed anyway except in the minds of Peters and Waterman (1982). Certainly the reality for many chief executives is a reality of leading without a clear expectation of what the outcome will look like. We do not know what will happen to public service when and if the market model peaks.

It could be that this comes as something of a relief. It gives us an opportunity to live with some ambiguities of a public service system which is trying to take on board the lessons of the market place. It allows for a revised form of professionalism to remerge. It permits diversity in management arrangements and in styles of management to begin to surface. It questions the value of enhanced user choice where the chosen is not available due to resource constraint. Above all it is a chance to create modes of service delivery which put empowerment back into our caring services, back into our service users and back into our communities. The last 50 years have demonstrated what happens when empowerment is bolted onto an inappropriate service delivery system. The empowering manager will be the one who works at the interface of organisations to create, not seamless, but jigsaw services for users. Learning to do that is arguably the business of managers in the 1990s.

REFERENCES

Hjern, B. and Porter, D.O. (1981), 'Implementation structures: a new kind of administrative analysis', in *Organizational Studies*, vol. 2/3, pp. 211–227

Leadbetter, C. (1991), 'Whose line is it anyway?', *Marxism Today*, July

Osbourne, D. and Gaebler, T. (1992), *Reinventing Government*, Wokingham: Addison-Wesley

Peters, T.J. and Waterman, R.H. (1982), *In Search of Excellence*, New York: Harper and Row

Index

Mintzberg, H., 7, 26, 95
Mishra, R., 10
mixed economy, 3, 10
mixed economy of care, 61, 62, 63
monetarism, 17
Mooney, 45
moral high ground, control of, 14
morale, 50
Morgan, G., 44
Morris, W., 45, 47
motivation, 50
multi-national conglomerates, 26

National Association for Care and
    Resettlement of Offenders
    (NACRO), 64
neo-classical economics, 17
network organisations, 97, 102–4,
    105–6
NHS, 69, 71, 106, 107
NHS and Community Care Act
    (1990), 64
Normann, R., 47, 93, 94

oil crisis, 23
operational management, 7
opportunism, 94
opposition, political, 15
opt-out arrangements, 66, 83
organic model of organisations, 52–3
organisational culture, 51
organisational learning, 52, 91
organisational theory, 42–56
Osborne, D., 107

paradigm, notion of, 17
part-time work, 21, 25
Parton, N., 35, 37
Patten, J., 93
performance contracts, 78, 81
periodisation, 17
PEST analysis, 91
Peters, T.J., 18, 51, 56, 107
planning, 84–90
    see also business planning; rational
        planning model

political accountability, 68–71
political approach to strategy, 94–5
political opposition, 15
political representation, 2–3
political trends, 11–16
politics, 2
Poor Law, 35
population, 23
Porter, D.O., 103
Porter, M.E., 92
portfolio approach, 92
poverty, 32, 37
principled management, 4, 5
private education, 21
private health care, 21
private-public debate, 60–3
Probation Service, 64–5
production
    assembly line, 45
    regionalisation of, 26
    small-batch, 27
production model of work
    organisation, 47, 48
professional bureaucracy, 97, 98,
    100–1, 102, 105
professional services, 26
professionals/professionalism, 12,
    26–7, 30, 40–1, 79, 98, 100
psychology and social work, 36
public expenditure, control of, 13,
    14, 17, 18, 59
public-private debate, 60–3
public representation, 70

quality assurance, 78, 81
quality of services, 69
Quinn, J.B., 7, 55, 94

race and employment, 24
racial inequality, 3, 22
rational approach to strategy, 90–2
rational planning model, 77
recession, 15, 17
regionalisation, 17
    of production, 26
Reilly, 45